ENDORSEMENTS

I0141306

I finished the book last night and it took me some places that evoke different emotions. I really liked the ending prayers after her specific prayer needs. I have to tell you, after the first two pages of "Derek" I already knew he was a narcissist… as was the person I married. It is my opinion narcissism is a result of mental illness and emotional brokenness—this was a good book. It's as if she was telling my story.

—Angela

I took a chance on it. Boy, am I glad I did! This book had my attention from beginning to end! I enjoyed her storytelling methods. It seemed as though these were real stories that had happened. I would recommend this book to any reader. It was a captivating read.

—Stacy

This book is an absolute treasure. There is so much wisdom and solid counsel packed into this author's story of love and betrayal. It will have you laughing through tears. This account of love (and loss) makes for an excellent book club read and will have you wondering when the movie will be released.

—Leslie

This book is wonderful…it's a must read! Reading this book helped me rethink my way of handling mentally abusive partners. Her storytelling was so real as if I was right there with her. Really enjoyed reading it…told a few of my friends that the book was great and they had to go and buy it!

—Genia

After You Say I Do Twice

TERESA SMITH

Copyright © 2019 by Teresa Smith

After You Say "I Do" Twice
by Teresa Smith

Printed in the United States of America

ISBN: 978-1-7336986-2-7

All rights reserved. No part of this document may be reproduced or transmitted in any form, by any means (electronic, photocopying, recording, or otherwise) without the written permission of the author.

Published by:
READY Publication, Gail Dudley
1491 Polaris Parkway, #81
Columbus, Ohio 43240 USA
www.GailDudley.com
www.ReadyPublication.com

Cover design by Dominiq Dudley

DEDICATION

I dedicate this book to women who have been married and divorced. You aren't alone. You are worthy and worth the love you deserve.

Sometimes we have to hurt before we heal.

Respectfully yours,

Teresa Smith

In Loving Memory

J. C. Smith Sr., Laura Smith, Willie Brown,
Annie Boyd, Dorothy Dotson, Bernice Smith,
Annie Harris, Lucille Harris, J. C. Smith Jr.,
Cephus Mitchell, Michael Smith

TABLE OF CONTENTS

INTRODUCTION

Every girl dreams about her wedding day. We are often taught getting married is one of the single most important things we can do in our lifetime.

We plan the wedding before we have a groom. We pick the colors, flowers, cake, food, music, dresses, bridesmaids, best woman, hairstyles, and possible venues.

We know where we will go for the honeymoon. We have prayed, fasted, strategized, and nothing but death will keep us from that altar.

What happens after you say I do?

CHAPTER ONE

MARRIAGE ISN'T A FAIRY TALE

We have given clear instructions to pounce on anyone who will respond to the dreaded statement, "Speak now or forever hold your peace." We are like a lioness protecting her cub. The actual ceremony lasts fifteen to twenty minutes, but the marriage is supposed to last a lifetime. This is supposed to be the best day of the rest of your life.

We have planned for the wedding, looked for wedding attire, lost a few pounds, cried, prayed, jumped, and hopped and skipped in hopes that our first marriage will be the only marriage. We have fantasized about how our husbands will treat us. He will be our knight in shining armor. He will be the protector and provider. In our hearts and minds, he was the one God sent just for you. Nevertheless, what happens after you say I do?

Lisa married young the first time. She married Jacob because she was pregnant. Lisa was ashamed and confused; therefore, she believed marriage was the only option. She liked Jacob but didn't love him. She didn't know love outside of her family. She was inexperienced when it came to men. Lisa didn't date in elementary or high school. Her first real boyfriend was in college, but that didn't last very long.

Lisa had the pleasure of watching family members who were married, until death did them part. Albeit, the marriages were boring and filled with all kinds of drama, but they honored their covenant. Lisa didn't know diddly-squat about men. How can you enter into a relationship without any knowledge of who and what a man is? It's very difficult.

Lisa wasn't in tune with her spiritual side. If she was, she would have prevented a loveless, uncaring, and heartless union. She now knows it was the voice of the Lord saying, "NO!" Warning comes before destruction, but Lisa didn't listen. Lisa proceeded regardless of the warning. Her marriage was filled with poverty, unpaid rent, hunger, mismanagement of money, repossessions, regrets, and lack of communication. There were all kinds of drama, and Lisa contributed to it.

Jacob wanted to be married because his parents were married for over fifty years, but he lacked the maturity to be a husband and Lisa lacked the maturity to be a wife. They were two people connected by covenant but working against each other. Jacob and Lisa decided she would be a stay-at-home mother. It was the worst mistake Lisa could have made. She was completely dependent upon Jacob for survival.

Jacob was so irresponsible with money. He liked to look good on the outside while there was no food or lights on the inside. Lisa was so confused because in all of her years growing up in Little Rock, Arkansas, she had never been without food or lights. Lisa's grandparents were providers.

Growing up, Lisa thought they were rich because they never went without. It was a shock to Lisa's system to have married the opposite of what she experienced growing up. Jacob maintained a job and he wanted wealth; however, Jacob spent a lot of time and money on get-rich-quick schemes. Lisa admired Jacob's desire to be rich, but his methods were shady. Wealth can be achieved by working, investing, and saving your money. Lisa learned the first week that marriage isn't a fairy tale, and you won't know that until you are in it. Lisa's beliefs and thoughts about marriage weren't aligning with the reality of marriage.

Lisa should have known Jacob wasn't the best candidate for a husband because when she moved from Little Rock, Arkansas, to Mobile, Alabama, Jacob had a picture of his ex-fiancée on the wall. Jacob didn't see anything wrong with the picture because his father and nephew were also in it. Jacob didn't take the picture down immediately. Lisa shrugged it off. In hindsight, it's completely disrespectful for any man or woman to have pictures of their exes on their wall when they are "trying" to move forward. It's a slap in the face to your new spouse.

It took a minute, but that is when Lisa learned that every goodbye ain't gone. Some people can physically move on with another person, but the heart wants who and what the heart wants. Lisa stayed and tried to be a wife. She even turned to religion for support. Lisa's belief in God didn't help her *situation* at all. Lisa was miserable.

Lisa became pregnant with baby number two. She just had to bring a second child into this dysfunction. After adding a second child to the equation, it increased the stress and pressure they were already experiencing. It's a good idea to get to know your spouse before you bring children into your dysfunction. Lack of money, children, and a loveless message are a recipe for divorce.

Jacob spent more time out of the house than with his family. Lisa never gave any thought to whether or not Jacob had an affair. She could care less. Lisa kicked herself for getting married and bringing two children into this mess. Children don't deserve to suffer because of their parents' disobedience. That's exactly what we do when we marry impulsively.

The Word tells us to be fruitful and multiply. Lisa wished the Bible was more clear. It would have been nice if the Scripture stated, "Be fruitful and multiply when you are ready for the responsibility financially, emotionally, and mentally." That's a whole other story.

CHAPTER TWO

NO COMMUNICATION KILLS A MARRIAGE

Fidelity isn't the only component that will keep a husband and wife together. Jacob tells everyone, "I didn't cheat on her." He didn't spend time with his wife and children. He didn't talk. He didn't pay bills on time. He didn't communicate. He was quiet and mumbled incoherent sentences. He wasn't able to articulate his displeasure until he was angry. He communicated clearly if he was angry.

He was consumed with his family members and their needs. He wouldn't wash a dish, take out the trash, or clean unless he was moving furniture around. They were miserable, and had Lisa stayed, she would have had an affair to break up the monotony. Lisa decided to leave because she had a candidate in mind.

Lisa decided enough was enough. She didn't want to try any longer. She was taking her children and leaving. There must be a better life than this. Jacob, like a lot of husbands, wasn't in tune with himself or his family. They give the best of themselves to people outside of the home. A lot of men are the best "husbands" to their coworkers, neighbors, family, and friends.

Lisa's neighbors admitted being jealous of her marriage because of the way Jacob bragged about their marriage and the way he treated his wife. Lisa was confused because she and

Jacob slept in separate rooms, and they rarely talked. Lisa kept telling Jacob to spend time with his children because he never knew if they would be there when he came home. Jacob said, "You aren't going anywhere. Where will you go? Who wants you? You are skinny, jacked-up teeth, and two children. You haven't worked. No one wants you." Jacob had this self-satisfying smile like he had won.

He had no clue the U-Haul truck was rented. Lisa had already gone to the police department and told them she wasn't kidnapping her children but was moving to Flint, Michigan, with family in order to escape a failed marriage, feelings of abandonment, and poverty. Jacob had underestimated his little, dumb wife. Jacob blames her cousin for breaking up their marriage. This thought showed he never knew his wife. She left because of Jacob's inability to provide for and protect his family. Lisa guessed it was easier for Jacob to blame someone else instead of looking inwardly.

Lisa couldn't think of a time that she and Jacob actually had an intimate conversation. Lisa didn't know Jacob's favorite color, food, song, or anything. She didn't know much about him at all. He rarely talked, and Lisa didn't press the issue. A lack of communication can lead to consistent negativity in interactions. Lisa and Jacob's nonverbal exchanges were equally ineffective. Poor communication can make one feel incompatible and frustrated with their spouse or partner. Lack of communication is a major component that leads to divorce. How do you get to know your spouse if you don't talk to each other?

CHAPTER THREE

A FRESH START

<hr>

Lisa and her children started over in Flint, Michigan. Her family criticized her for leaving a "diamond in the rough." Jacob "wanted his family back." Lisa was confused because she didn't understand his definition of family. Did he want his family back because he was ashamed they left? After all, he had this public image of being the best husband. Did he want his family back because his goal was to be married one time? That was his goal.

Most people go into a marriage believing the first marriage will be their only marriage. However, it doesn't always work out like that. Why want something that he didn't appreciate or didn't help cultivate? He wasn't ready to be a husband nor was Lisa ready to be a wife. Jacob is a good father, but he wasn't ready for the responsibility that came with having a family. Marriage is for selfless people. Lisa felt sorry for Jacob because she had moved on. She wishes him well because it appears he's still holding on to what was.

Regardless of what he wanted, Lisa was done with Jacob. She had no desire to be anything to him or with him except coparenting their children. Jacob probably thought he was the victim of a wife who left him. They were both victims. Jacob may have witnessed a two-parent home where the mom stayed home and the dad worked, but Jacob didn't know how to manage his money.

Jacob, like most people, was infatuated with being "married" rather than actually "cultivating the marriage." Lisa was no psychic, but she knew her marriage with Jacob would have been filled with overspending, repossessions, evictions, little to no food, extreme poverty, constantly begging others for help, poor money management, no growth, and misery.

Marriage is more than "wanting to stay married because your parents were married for fifty years." Lisa was conflicted because the Scriptures do say for "better or worse." She didn't know who or what determined worse, but to be in the home with a person you don't love and who doesn't love you is like a slow death. It was pointless. It was like watching a horror movie in slow motion. Lisa was worried about the effects divorce would have on their children .

Lisa had friends who were single parents and their children were fine. Plus, she had family members who were the product of divorce, and their children were fine. Children are resilient, and they will eventually be fine. Lisa packed a few clothes, took a 13-inch television with a VHI attached to it, and $36 in order to begin her new life. They took US 90, onto I-165 N towards Montgomery, through Louisville, and merging unto I-75, crossing into Ohio. There it was, the sign for US-23 towards Flint. The drive was fifteen hours and nineteen minutes. Lisa stepped out of the U-Haul and exhaled. She felt free. The past five years had been stressful and hellish. Those years were a blur, and better yet, they were over.

Two weeks after moving to Flint, Lisa was teaching at a Montessori school. She enjoyed that job because her children, Caden and Ashley, could attend the after-school program for free. The girls would ask for their father, and Lisa would tell them he would be able to visit them. They were too young to understand.

Lisa's family tried to make her go back for the sake of the children. Oh, ye hypocrites; none of you stayed with your significant others for the "sake of your children." Lisa's family didn't know the extent of the hell she had endured because they were only aware of bits and pieces. She wasn't about to feel guilty for starting over.

Throughout the years, Lisa spent time dating different guys, but nothing really panned out. She was empty, and her feelings of emptiness and loneliness grew with every sexual encounter. She was missing something, not someone. All of the sex and casual relationships didn't mean a thing. Lisa was bored. She didn't want to go back to Jacob, but she wanted a relationship.

Lisa didn't want to be in a committed relationship; she wanted to be in a relationship that she deemed healthy. One without any attachments or commitments. Lisa's mentality was warped. She had taken on the mind-set of a man. She wasn't acting like a lady. She "hit it and quit it." She dated guys who didn't have steady careers, drug dealers, gang members, guys with girlfriends, and guys with wives. Nothing mattered because Lisa was lost and living recklessly. After being married, she came to the conclusion that it was better to have sex, and send the guy home.

Years went by and Lisa became tired of the impact divorce had on her children. Don't get it twisted; she wasn't going back to Jacob. She wanted to be close in order for them to coparent successfully. Lisa moved from Flint, MI, to Mobile, AL, in order to be actively engaged with her children. She hoped Jacob was over her, because there was something about him she didn't like. All she wanted was for Caden and Ashley to have the best of both parents.

Lisa began working a series of low-paying jobs just to get by. She stayed single and free for a little while. She started serial dating, but there went that nagging voice. She ignored that nagging voice with every sexual encounter. She was empty married and empty dating. What's the problem? Lisa had always dreamed of being a nun and living a celibate life. Was her destiny destroyed because she got pregnant and married? Is she feeling empty because none of these men are a godsend?

She sank deeper and deeper into an abyss. Her choice of men became more and more pathetic. She experienced women throwing bottles at her car, banging on her door, and a series of threatening calls. She was stalked by a lover's girlfriend and her entire family from Bastrop, Louisiana. The girlfriend of one man found Lisa's information by going through his phone.

After a failed marriage and failed relationships, Lisa knew she was a part of the problem. She had enough of lies, being harassed, feeling cheated, and most of all, not loving herself enough to make better choices. Lisa sat on her sofa and decided all the empty relationships, sexcapades, and low self-esteem were enough. She was fed up with not being enough. She repented for all her sins and asked God to forgive her for every bad decision and act she had participated in. She threw away her mattress and everything that connected her with any man she had slept with. She didn't want any reminders of her former self. She wanted to be free of everything that had her in bondage.

CHAPTER FOUR

A QUEST FOR FREEDOM

Lisa was on a quest for freedom, self-love, and reconnecting with the only one whose love never fails—Jesus. Lisa's thoughts became clearer, and her life became peaceful. There was no confusion and no mixed messages. Every now and then someone from her past would call. Lisa decided that she wasn't going to dance with God and hold hands with the devil. It was best to forego all communication with anyone from the past. She made a decision to cut all ties, including email. It was time to let the dead bury the dead. So the journey began.

The girls were young adults and independent. Lisa had accomplished what she set out to do. She wanted to see her daughters grow up. Lisa didn't particularly like living in Mobile, AL. The job market wasn't the best. Lisa completed her undergraduate degree but she couldn't find work that paid well. Two years later, Lisa completed her graduate degree and took a lucrative job in Oklahoma City, Oklahoma.

This felt like déjà vu, Lisa packing up the U-Haul and moving to a new city eleven years later. She wanted to get to Oklahoma City a week before beginning her job in order to get settled in her new place. So she started out on US-90 onto Moffett Road/US-98 crossing into Mississippi. She merged onto I-59 N, US-49 N towards Jackson, and eventually I-235 N into Oklahoma City.

Lisa began working at Cedar Ridge Behavioral Hospital on May 3. She was living the dream. She had the salary she wanted and was finally living the lifestyle she had longed for. She was reading the Word, praying, fasting, and tithing. Lisa had found a church and was overall happy. She connected with some powerful women in ministry and was attending women's conferences and prayer breakfasts. Lisa was sold out to God.

She woke up studying the Word of God and went to sleep studying the Word of God. She was listening to inspirational CDs, reading books on spiritual warfare, God's favor, etc. Lisa was hungry for the Word of God and God's will for her life. She was attending soaking sessions with church members and learning so much about God and His Word. Lisa was content in all things.

She was jovial and attended to attract all sorts of people. Lisa built a relationship with some mature women at her church. All of the women had been married for over thirty years. Some were on their second and third marriages. Nevertheless, they were married over thirty years. The women began praying for Lisa to have a husband who would protect her anointing.

As time went on, that constant question became, "Where is your husband?" It went from one extreme to the next. "She must be gay or have some homosexual tendencies." Lisa had been celibate for several years and people acted like that was the end of the world.

Other Christians frowned upon Lisa's decision. Some said, "That is Old Testament law. Jesus paid it all." Lisa was aware that some of her friends were trying to get her to fall because they had fallen into temptation. She was committed to her relationship with God and wanted to serve God with her whole heart, mind, body, and soul.

Years went by, and Lisa went out on a few dates here and there. It never failed. After one or two dinner dates, the men started talking about sex. Lisa began to give up hope that a man would wait to have sex until after marriage. She attended concerts, plays, operas, and she got the chance to listen to a one- hundred-piece orchestra.

It became very noticeable that Lisa was alone. Everywhere she went she was surrounded by couples. The desire to be in a relationship began to rise. *I love God, but do I want to be the cat lady? Do I want to have a house full of animals and grow old alone?*

Lisa was fearful about getting into a serious relationship because outside of work, her life was drama free. Lisa heard a televangelist say, "If you want to be a wife, you have to act like one, even in your singleness." So she began studying the purpose of marriage, the role of a wife, how to be a good wife, a praying wife, etc.

Lisa wrote the vision and made it plain. She was encouraged to write down the qualities and characteristics she wanted in a husband:

1. He must be saved.
2. He must love God more than himself.
3. He must have a legal job.
4. He must be over six feet tall.
5. He must be attractive.
6. He can't have children under eighteen years old.
7. He must be clean and like to smell good.
8. He must not be violent or abusive.
9. He must be a good communicator.
10. He must be willing to forsake all others.

Lisa didn't know what else to add to the list. She had reservations on whether or not that would actually help with selecting a mate. She joined married groups on social media. If God blessed her with a husband, she was determined not to fail at another marriage. Lisa would be a better wife, friend, listener, and helpmeet.

Lisa had a different revelation about the Proverbs 31 woman. She admired her, but her interpretation of that passage was a woman who married a wealthy man who provided her with handmaidens. Those handmaidens helped her to manage the household.

Some of us aren't blessed enough to marry into wealth. No woman can singlehandedly perform all of those tasks without drinking or having a nervous breakdown. It's good to take care of the home, but a wife has to take care of herself in the process.

Marriage became like a carrot that dangled in front of Lisa. Should she consider marriage in the future; should she not? It was unnerving, because marriage shouldn't be entered into lightly. Was fear keeping her from dating? Was she afraid that lightning would strike twice? Lisa had always joked about being the black Elizabeth Taylor, with one marriage down and seven more to go.

She knew she wasn't a nun because she still had the desire to be one with a man. She really enjoyed knowing her partner in a biblical way. Was she missing out on something being single? Should she simply stay single? Marriage is work. If you end up with the wrong spouse, marriage will hit you like a tsunami. It will eventually bury you alive.

The church tells you to get to know yourself, being single is best, you can do so much alone, you can get to know God and work for Him, and life is so much better as a single woman. In the back of her mind, Lisa still had a desire to get married. Her desire grew due to her work environment. It was difficult coming home alone after dealing with a psychotic supervisor. Lisa enjoyed talking to God but she wanted to talk to a companion. There was no comfort.

It was hard, harsh, and lonely. Lisa felt isolated. She had no one to comfort her when she was sad. The stress on her body was excessive and there was no one to rub her shoulders or feet. Evangelist Clark said, "Singleness can be a gift." Lisa said, "According to Scripture, 'Two are better than one, because they have a good return for their labor' " (Ecclesiastes 4:9). Lisa decided that she was a good woman and deserved to be a wife. Somewhere, there was a love just for her.

A couple of years later, Jacob moved to Oklahoma and right down the street from Lisa. Lisa said, "Really God, if Jacob is the one, I would rather remain single all the days of my life." Different people believed that God sent her ex-husband to reconcile. Lisa felt strongly that it was a trick from the enemy. Everyone won't have Hosea and Gomer's story. Lisa wasn't taking on any Home Depot projects and building a man.

Family and friends kept saying Jacob needed a woman to teach him stability, or he needed her to give him direction. Lisa felt, God created man, and it wasn't a woman's job to rebuild him. Jacob and his supporters better get a life, and that life didn't include restoration with her. Lisa wondered if people had been filling Jacob's head up with the line, "We belong together."

People planted seeds and those seeds grew into a movie that one plays over and over again. In other words, people will give you false hope. Some of Lisa's friends even tried to get her to reconsider reconciling with Jacob. Lisa didn't reveal what she secretly said about those friends.

Lisa was interested in dating, but she wasn't going backwards. Her coworkers encouraged her to create an account on an internet dating site, and that is where she met Derek. Derek had all of the qualities she liked. They communicated via the internet before exchanging numbers. Derek and Lisa talked and talked. Derek was a good communicator and listener. The more they talked, the more they found out they had a lot in common.

Lisa and Derek had attended Central High School in Little Rock, AR. They even knew some of the same people. Lisa felt comfortable with Derek because they shared familiar history. However, she was leery of Derek's victim's mentality. She noticed that he blamed everybody for his failures, sadness, heartbreak, etc.

He never admitted doing anything wrong to anyone. Any "horrible" thing that could have been done wrong was done to him. That should have been a big, red flag. Nevertheless, Lisa had a way of looking past faults and finding the good in people.

Lisa and Derek agreed to discuss their failed marriages one time and one time only in an effort to see if they had learned from their past mistakes. They discussed their dreams, childhood, careers, and relationship goals to include marriage. They discussed their expectations.

They had a similar upbringing. Both were raised by their aunt and uncle. Unlike Derek, Lisa was healed from her parents' choice not to raise her. She loved living with her aunt and uncle and the relationships and closeness she had with all of her cousins and wouldn't trade it for the world.

Derek was still struggling with being rejected by his parents. He often discussed never understanding why his parents didn't want him. Lisa encouraged him to seek help. Derek believed he was fine. Lisa justified again, "He seems all right." Lisa's gut was screaming, "Warning! Proceed with caution." Lisa and Derek agreed to date and be exclusive.

They talked every day, sometimes up to five times, and the conversation flowed for hours. Lisa woke up to good-morning messages and went to sleep to good-night text messages. Derek was extremely thoughtful and very sweet on the surface.

Derek and Lisa studied the Word and prayed together. Both were divorced with adult children. Derek had an adult daughter and son, and Lisa had two adult daughters. Derek and Lisa were gainfully employed. Both were tired of dating, meeting family members, and starting over. He wanted to be a husband; she wanted to be a wife. They agreed to get married, regardless of their three-month courtship. Lisa's rationale was, Derek is saved, mature in age, a minister, and desired to be married, so it could work if both parties were sure this was what they wanted, right?

They agreed to fast and pray in order to hear from God. What God did reveal in Lisa's dream was a woman looming over Derek's life. There was a clear visual of a woman Derek was attached to spiritually and emotionally. The woman didn't have a face in Lisa's dream, but she was whispering in Derek's ear and he was smiling.

That same week a church mother said, "I don't know how to say this, but I know you are getting married. God showed me a witchcraft spirit hovering over Derek, and there is a woman he's connected to. Please pray, daughter."

God was still silent. Lisa and Derek continued talking. They discussed the prophetic, speaking in tongues, and the fruits of the Spirit. Derek said, "We had a prophet come to our church and he was rude. He asked me if I was living for Christ and I said yes. This so-called prophet told me I was trying but I'm not there yet. He made me mad."

Lisa said, "Warning comes before destruction, and the prophet's job is to warn God's people."

Derek said, "He was judging me ,and only God can judge me."

Lisa asked, "You don't like correction, do you?"

Derek didn't respond.

Lisa asked, "Were you living right when the prophet told you that?"

Derek hesitated and said, "I was sleeping with my girlfriend."

Lisa said, "At no time did you think the man of God was trying to correct you? You took offense to the warning." She continued, "Years ago, I was prophesied to by a woman of God who lowered her microphone and told me to get out of the bed with that man. No one should have known about that man because he was in another state. I didn't get mad or offended. I actually got out of that relationship. Guess what? He was married."

The word "pride" dropped in Lisa's spirit. She said, "I hope you aren't afraid of the prophetic, because I've been told I am a seer. I've actually seen things since I was younger, but I didn't know what any of it meant. Two years ago, Evangelist Clark and Lady Yvette told me on two separate occasions that I was a seer and the other one said I was prophetic. Is that going to be a problem for you?"

Derek said, "Oh no, I understand. Our church has prophetic people in it."

Lisa already knew she was going to inform Derek of her dream. She asked, "Derek, are you emotionally connected to anyone? Because emotional connection is detrimental to moving forward."

Derek said, "No, I'm over any woman. Shoot, I'm ready to move forward."

Lisa had that bubbling up feeling in the pit of her stomach. She knew Derek was lying, but she gave him the benefit of the doubt. Lisa thought something wasn't right, but Derek was so convincing. She chose to believe Derek because all of us lie, right?

Derek laid it on really thick after Lisa told him about the dream. He became so attentive. He was very courteous and kind. If Lisa had been paying attention, she would've known it was all a game. She asked Derek to discuss how he managed his emotions whenever he became angry.

Derek said, "I don't do drama."

Lisa responded, "That's not what I asked." She explained, "I get angry, I throw a tantrum, but I'm fine within minutes, and the anger is over."

Derek said, "I like to talk things over."

Lisa said, "Derek, I don't hold grudges. My grandmother taught us to not let the sun go down on our wrath. I didn't know that was Scripture until I got older."

Derek replied, "I don't hold grudges either."

Lisa purposely attempted to provoke Derek in order to get a reaction. She had always been told you can tell a lot about a person by the way they respond in anger. Derek never responded in anger.

Lisa thought this guy was too good to be true. Derek spoke Lisa's love language. Lisa loved to talk, and Derek was a talker. He didn't do much to affirm Lisa, but he didn't mind talking.

She loved that he responded to her text messages and showed her some semblance of respect. Lisa would often hear women complain about how men don't respond to text messages. Derek responded to text messages and missed calls faster than the speed of lightning.

CHAPTER FIVE

DON'T BE UNEQUALLY YOKED

Derek didn't mind telling Lisa of his whereabouts. He didn't believe he was "checking in." He expressed it was a sign of respect. He exuded some excellent qualities. He communicated well, was slow to get angry, didn't hold grudges, responded to messages and phone calls in a timely manner, had a legal job, and was a believer. Derek was a Christian, and the Bible tells us not to be unequally yoked with unbelievers.

Lisa laid it all out there. She informed Derek that one of her best friends was a guy and his name was Richard. Lisa and Richard had been friends since they were seventeen, and she wanted to continue the friendship without any conflict. Derek stated, "That is fine, because I am secure."

He then stated he had three female friends; two of them Lisa knew, and one male friend. Lisa informed Derek that she had more than four friends and tended to attract all types of people. Derek said, "You won't need anyone but me. I don't like to be around a lot of people. My ex-wife used to love to be around people too." Red flags were popping up everywhere, but Lisa ignored them all.

Regardless of the red flags, Lisa rationalized that God would be at the center of their relationship. However, Lisa waited before sharing intimate details about her life. She decided it was time to tell Derek that she has been celibate for seven years. Derek said, "That is good. I don't mind waiting." Hindsight is 20/20 because Derek stated he could wait but didn't admit being celibate. Nevertheless, Derek impressed Lisa by saying he was willing to wait.

They discussed their failed marriages, and Lisa noticed something that made her uncomfortable. Derek blamed his ex-wife for the dissolution of their marriage, whereas Lisa said she didn't love or like her ex, and both of them could have used some help in order to become better spouses. Lisa informed Derek that she wished she had remained celibate and never married, but she got her children out of the deal. She tried not to focus on Jacob; nor did she like discussing the past.

Derek lived in the past. He constantly talked about how badly his ex-wife treated him; how she lied, manipulated, and used him. Derek credited himself with his ex-wife's success. As a matter of fact, Derek would rant about every woman he met and how manipulative and broken each one was. This made Lisa question Derek's honesty, but not enough to end the relationship. Derek claimed he was loyal and people usually hurt him first.

Lisa contemplated but had to ask Derek one question. She inquired, "So Derek, every woman you met dogged you out, which I don't believe. You claim your ex-wife cheated on you, but women don't typically cheat unless the man cheats first; if there is neglect on the part of the man, or she's a whore when you get with her. I don't believe you have been a victim in all of your relationships. You may be doing something you aren't aware of, and you don't want to change, because I believe it takes two people to ruin the relationship in most cases. Unless one person is extremely selfish and just wants out."

It was more of an observation than a question. Lisa wasn't comfortable with Derek's version of the stories, because women typically don't leave "perfect" and "good" men, and

Derek presented himself as perfect. He often described himself as a "good" man. Derek claimed he paid for everything, and his ex-wife didn't want for anything. Why would a wife leave a husband like that? Either his ex-wife was selfish, or Derek was delusional.

Lisa never heard Derek assume accountability for anything. That should have been a red flag, but Lisa tended to overlook those molehills. Derek and Lisa continued talking but kept their relationship relatively a secret. The more they talked, the more comfortable Lisa became.

Derek wasn't as perfect as he believed, but the two shared similar relationship goals, morals, and values. Derek's children didn't talk to him until they needed something and neither did Lisa's. However, all four of their children were over eighteen and not completely dependent upon their parents. Lisa was happy she wouldn't have to deal with baby-momma drama.

Derek wasn't the finest thing walking, but he was attractive. Lisa and Derek discussed marriage but he didn't propose to her. It was more like a scene from *Sex and the City* when Big told Carrie he wouldn't mind being married to her. It was nothing to brag about. After talking on the phone, Lisa and Derek decided to do a meet and greet.

Lisa informed Richard that she and Derek were going to meet face-to-face. Lisa resided in Oklahoma City and Derek resided in Arlington, TX. The two cities are three hours apart. Richard said, "Don't trust him. Don't be alone with him. Put yourself in a safe environment because some men don't respect celibacy, and I don't want you to be disrespected."

Lisa said, "I've gone without sex this long. Surely one week around a man won't cause me to fall."

Richard said, "Truthfully, you are probably celibate because you have been busy with work and school and haven't been around men. Just be careful because we (men) are slick. I just don't want you to get hurt."

Seven years of celibacy went down the tube in one night. Derek began caressing and rubbing on Lisa. Richard's words resonated, "Don't trust him." Derek continued with sexual advances towards Lisa. Lisa chose flesh over God. Lisa slept with a man who said he would wait. She woke up guilt ridden, and Derek had that smug look on his face. He actually said, "You didn't try to stop me."

Lisa realized her error. She began feeling all of the emotions after having sex such as shame, filth, and confusion. She felt dirty and realized why she stopped having sex. "He doesn't respect you or himself," were the words resonating over and over again. "Run, Lisa, run. You compromised your beliefs for sex. He isn't the one God has chosen for you." Lisa didn't listen. All of the classic signs were present. She repented and moved forward.

Shortly after their sexual encounter, Lisa was asked to speak at a women's conference, and the topic was "Women in Waiting." Condemnation and conviction were beating her like a drum. She told Derek she could not go before women and talk about waiting after they just had sex. She said, "I'm going to tell the women that I was celibate, but broke it."

Derek said, "It ain't their business. Don't tell anyone. Most Christians do have sex." He encouraged Lisa to be quiet and not tell anyone, and, "God forgives."

Lisa always got this feeling in the pit of her stomach when something or someone wasn't right. That bubbling in her gut was there again. Something wasn't right, but she couldn't put her finger on it. There was something destructive behind Derek's eyes, but she couldn't detect it. She admonished herself silently. Lisa was in spiritual warfare.

She gave her spiritual virginity to a man who couldn't wait. His words were, "I don't mind waiting." The signs were there. She ignored them. She could have said no. Lisa had one big character flaw as she tended to "go along to get along." She was too passive and too forgiving.

Lisa's logic was that she had to get married to undo the dirty feeling she had incurred despite that sick feeling in the pit of her stomach. She knew in the back of her mind that Derek was all talk and had created this external personality that "he was as close to God as Jesus." She spent seven years in covenant with God and God only. Her body was a complete act of worship.

How could Lisa judge Derek as a lukewarm Christian, because she was one as well? Derek had been in and out of the bed with women, and Lisa had been celibate, but one slip made her just as bad as him. This wasn't good. She wanted to confess that she had slept with Derek, but he coaxed her into not telling anyone.

Lisa did confess to a few close girlfriends, who prayed and encouraged her not to walk around with the guilt and shame. Rhonda stated, "You may as well marry him because all of us fall. He sounds like he has some good qualities."

Lisa's elderly neighbor stated, "You know what you want and so does he. Put God first and move forward. Forgive yourself."

So much support. So much encouragement.

Lisa and Derek agreed that she would move to Arlington, TX, after they got married. In the meantime, Lisa decided to speak at the women's conference. She said, "I'm not a public speaker, and my nerves are shot. I haven't done everything right, but when I say there are benefits in waiting, I'm speaking from the depths of my soul. You don't have to deal with guilt and shame. The spiritual warfare that comes after premarital sex is exhausting. While waiting, we should stay busy with the things of the Lord and don't forget to enjoy life in the process. Ruth was busy gleaning when Boaz noticed her. Adam was busy naming animals and working the earth before God created Eve. I beg of you to wait."

Lisa begged the women to hold on to their bodies and not to let anyone make them compromise. "Work on yourself before your husband comes. There is a quote I love, 'Waiting for God isn't laziness. Waiting for God isn't going to sleep. Waiting for God isn't the abandonment of effort. Waiting for God means, first, activity under command; second, readiness for any new command that may come; third, the ability to do nothing until the command is given' (G. Campbell Morgan). Waiting on God is the ultimate test because that means we trust God's decision for our lives."

That little voice said, *Did Lisa really trust God? If so, she wouldn't have fallen so quickly.* "Thanks for listening, and I pray something I said blessed someone on tonight. Amen and amen."

There was a Q & A at the end of the conference. All of the women and men who attended were looking for love. Married women and single women attended the conference. There were people who had been married and divorced multiple times.

One woman's testimony shook Lisa to the core. She was married to a pastor who was verbally and physically abusive. He was a serial cheater, and the only reason she stayed for as long as she did was to prevent a church hurt. She was miserable, but she had to pretend. Lisa thought of Derek while the lady was speaking. Is that evil glance behind his eyes one of an abuser? After all, he's a minister!

Lisa called Derek on the ride home. Derek asked, "How did it go?"

Lisa said, "It went well." She still felt like she deceived people.

Derek asked, "How many people do you think are having premarital sex? These gospel singers and preachers are having sex."

She heard, *Run. Lisa. Run. He's no good for you. Run.* She began justifying. Is it fear? Is it a commitment phobia? What is it? Lisa said, "Derek, you haven't been faithful to God, and I have fallen since meeting you. Don't you have any remorse?"

Derek said, "It's not that. People sin all of the time."

Lisa said, "I can't help but feel like I cheated on my best friend, meaning God."

Derek said, "God understands."

Lisa asked, "Derek, are you sure you aren't marrying me to get even with your ex-girlfriend?"

Derek didn't respond. His silence was deafening.

CHAPTER SIX

MARRIAGE ISN'T A CURE

"I don't want to be a rebound date," Lisa said matter-of-factly.

Derek replied. "Why would you say something like that? I'm not stuck on anyone. That relationship has been over and I'm ready to move forward."

The more Derek talked, the more Lisa's gut stirred. "We had sex more than once before getting married after we agreed not to," Lisa cried out to Derek, and she told him she could not be used for sex. She wasn't comfortable being a lukewarm a Christian. This wasn't where she saw herself and not the type of man she envisioned for herself. This wasn't what she wanted—sex without commitment.

Lisa said she couldn't continue like that. They decided to set the wedding date earlier than planned. It was better to marry than to burn with passion, right? Wrong. Marriage wasn't a cure for lust, as Lisa would soon find out.

Lisa rationalized that this would be a new thing. They screwed up, so now it was time to make it right in the eyes of the Lord. They decided they would get married in Arkansas. Lisa was forthcoming with Derek. She informed him that Jacob and their two daughters had moved to Oklahoma and currently lived down the street. Lisa asked, "Are you going to be okay with that?"

Derek replied, "Yes. I'm secure with myself."

Lisa later found out Derek didn't care that Jacob lived down the street from her because he lived four houses down from his ex-wife.

Lisa remembered a wise woman saying, "Men move on, but they don't move away," or something like that. She believed the statement meant men could jump from relationship to relationship and still be tied to the last woman.

The ceremony would be small, and they would have a big reception later to include family and friends. Derek didn't want their week to be flooded with too many family members because their time was precious. He was loud and clear by saying, "We don't need to invite a lot of family because we will only have one week together, and I want to spend that time with you."

Lisa told her dad, brother, and cousins not to worry about attending the ceremony. They both had family in Arkansas. Lisa detected a glimpse of a control freak, but it was very subtle and laced behind laughter. Lisa's gut was bubbling, but she was determined to get through the ceremony.

A few family members and friends showed up to support them. People were laughing and talking, but Derek sat there, disengaged from the group. Lisa attributed it to nerves. Derek was visibly disengaged and staring at the wall. Lisa thought maybe he was nervous, but the look on his face was sheer tension.

Derek had that same exasperated look that Jerry Maguire had when he was marrying Dorothy. Lisa sighed. She had come too far, and there was no turning back. As the minister was reading the vows, she became sick to her stomach. She always got that bubbly feeling in the pit of her stomach when something wasn't right. *Should she back out now?*

Every time Lisa had those feelings, she would be right about a person or situation. That sick feeling in the pit of her stomach prevented her from going into a store, and she avoided being in the middle of a robbery that resulted in murder.

That sick feeling prevented her from accepting a drink at a party and prompted her to leave that party early, only to find out a young lady was sexually assaulted later that night. That same bubbly feeling was there. Lisa's legs became so wobbly until she almost fell. She was visibly shaken, but clowned around in order to prevent it from being noticed.

CHAPTER SEVEN

ZERO AFFECTION

Is Derek the best candidate for a spouse? Is she making another huge mistake? Derek was focused on the minister throughout the ceremony. He didn't look in Lisa's direction until Lisa asked if he was marrying her or the minister. They both said I do, and so it began.

The newlyweds went out to eat with friends and family, and Derek wasn't engaged in any of the conversation. He spent the entire time texting on his phone. Immediately after saying I do, he wasn't attentive, and there was zero affection between two people who just got married. His behavior was stale. Derek only engaged in conversation with his son and nephew. To Lisa, it felt like they'd been married for years instead of hours.

Lisa was nervously happy and decided to make the best of the situation. She looked at Derek, and a feeling of dread overwhelmed her. She would find out later that her best friend's boyfriend had been studying Derek's behavior the entire time, and he wasn't pleased. Lisa had this sinking feeling that this marriage would end soon. Derek was cold. Lisa kept looking at him and there was no emotion. Something wasn't right. In time, the truth would reveal itself.

Friday evening, Derek's aunt cooked a big meal for the married couple. Derek said, "We aren't going to stay long because we only have three more days together."

Lisa said, "Let's stay a couple of hours and go to the movies or do something fun."

Derek agreed, "Two hours will be the maximum."

They drove to Derek's aunt's house, and Lisa enjoyed the view on the drive. She loved the country, going home to Arkansas, and overlooking the fields and country homes. The environment was peaceful and quaint and the people were friendly and welcoming. Yes, Lisa loved coming home; she enjoyed the food and company.

Lisa observed Derek to be distant but more involved with his family. He was ignoring her. There was absolutely no affection between two people who just got married. Derek was busy talking to everyone except her. Lisa smiled and realized that she had made another mistake. "Dang, you just aren't good at this."

One day after being married, Lisa missed being single. Heck, Lisa gave herself more attention than Derek. Derek ate and went outside to talk to the neighbors. A few of Lisa's friends and family came over to eat dinner, but Derek remained outside the entire time. Lisa was ready to go after a few hours, but Derek wasn't ready to go.

Derek and Lisa's visit extended from two to eight hours. Lisa was slightly perturbed because her family wanted to be there to support her. The entire time Lisa was thinking this man completely dismissed her family by saying, "We are going to spend this time together." Lisa became pissed, declaring it wasn't going to be a one-sided marriage where his family was more important than hers type of deal.

Derek didn't even want to invite their two mutual friends because he said Emily was jealous. Derek believed Emily was jealous because her boyfriend was still legally married and hadn't proposed to her. Derek didn't want that negative energy around him and finally decided it was time to leave.

Lisa was angry and told Derek on the ride back to the hotel, but she didn't yell or speak in an aggressive tone. She said, "Derek, you specifically said we were going to stay for a couple of hours. You know everything shuts down in Arkansas at 10 p.m. If we were going home together, I wouldn't be upset, but we are going to different states."

Derek said, "I was trying to let you and the women get acquainted."

Lisa said, "You and I need to get acquainted." At that point she knew she had made a big mistake.

Derek was seething. He tried to hide it, but the look in his eyes told a different story. She knew this marriage would only get worse. Lisa apologized for being angry but hoped Derek understood her stance on dismissing her family. She said, "I could have pretended my feelings didn't matter, but I'm not going to be a prisoner in this marriage. I want us to be able to talk about anything, forgive, reach an understanding, and move forward."

Chapter Eight

Simple Sex

Lisa initiated small talk, because she was over yesterday's experience. Derek didn't respond. She wanted to enjoy the rest of their "honeymoon." Shortly afterwards Derek said, "You should have told me you were ready to go. You don't assume accountability or responsibility for anything."

Lisa replied, "Next time, I'll say something. You have my word on that."

Lisa and Derek made a truce. They played spades, laughed, and watched television. They fought it out and talked it out. Lisa thought it was over. Little did she know, Derek held grudges and would make her pay. Derek requested Richard's phone number "so they could talk." At that moment, Lisa was convinced Derek was controlling.

She didn't respond, nor did she provide him with her best friend's phone number. Richard was her best friend, not Derek's. Lisa didn't ask, nor did she want Derek's friend's contact information. She thought that was odd. She told him Richard had been her friend since they were seventeen years old, and she wasn't about to hand him over to Derek. Derek's best friend was a woman and Lisa didn't want her number either.

They spent a quiet evening not really talking. Derek spent the entire evening sulking. Lisa didn't provide Derek with

Richard's number, and he was ticked off. Lisa teased, "How long will you sulk? Make love to your wife." They had sex, but lovemaking didn't occur. Lisa didn't feel any connection to her husband. It was plain and simple sex. Most couples couldn't get enough of each other after they were married. Derek was more aggressive and sexually satisfying before marriage.

Lisa woke up, expecting to connect intimately with her husband before they headed back home. Derek was already up and dressed. He gave Lisa a peck on the cheek and was out the door. Derek went back to Texas and Lisa went back to Oklahoma. They talked minimally on the drive home.

Derek's son had attended the ceremony. Lisa made a statement and asked a question, "Derek, you weren't comfortable talking to me on the drive to Arkansas and now you aren't comfortable talking to me on the ride home. Are you having a difficult time talking to me in front of your son? Geesh, man. You were married to his mother, and if you can't talk to your current wife in front of him, then Houston, we have a problem."

Derek was extremely quiet and told Lisa he would call her after he dropped his son off. After Derek dropped him off, he called Lisa and chatted like normal.

Lisa thought to herself, *This man wears two faces*. Lisa didn't have a problem talking to Derek in front of her children, but clearly Derek had a problem engaging with her in front of his children. That was weird. Heck, the entire relationship was weird.

Lisa made plans to move to Texas, but she had to find a job first. She had been single and providing for her own needs for more than twenty years. She wasn't about to move with a husband and not have a source of income. Lisa was impulsive for marrying a stranger; however, she wasn't going to be financially dependent upon Derek.

Lisa thought, *Adam and Eve didn't date and were married after one night, but that worked for Adam and Eve. Adam was a provider. Lisa and Derek are tainted.* Immediately after going back to their respective homes, Derek changed drastically. He was no longer answering the phone as promptly as he had been. There weren't any good-morning or good-night text messages. Lisa knew Derek was also dealing with uncertainty and acted impulsively. He had become even more distant.

Two weeks after being married, Lisa's best friend called to inquire about the status of their marriage. Lisa said, "I'm not aware of any major concerns."

Joyce worked with Derek's cousin, who asked what was going on in the marriage. Joyce stated, "I told Derek's cousin that the only thing she knows is that y'all live too far apart." Joyce continued, "Derek told his cousin he wasn't happy, and marriage wasn't all that."

Lisa said, "Derek has been distant, but I didn't know he wasn't happy."

Joyce asked, "What happened?"

Lisa said, "I discussed my displeasure with spending all of our time with his family and not with each other."

Joyce asked, "Derek didn't understand that?"

Lisa said, "Apparently not. I thought the whole thing was over, but I guess not."

Joyce said, "Derek's cousin said she was concerned about him being with you, because he's a good guy. I took offense to that, and I told her my friend is a good girl."

Lisa told Joyce she didn't understand why Derek's cousin was trying to judge her, because she was sleeping with a married man, and that married man happened to be Lisa's cousin. Lisa felt Derek's cousin should worry about her own bedroom. Lisa said, "Women are always saying their brother, uncle, father, son, cousin are good men. How do they know? Have they slept with them? That irks me, because what is the definition of a good man? One who ignores his wife and complains about not being happy after two weeks, which means he was never happy?"

Lisa continued, "Why has Derek placed the responsibility on me to maintain his happiness? We are responsible for our own happiness. That burden is too heavy to carry." Lisa told Joyce she could relay that message if she liked and acknowledged, "I made a mistake by marrying Derek. He's meaner than he pretended to be. Derek is the type that likes the newness of a relationship. The high is gone and now he has flatlined. At the first sign of trouble he's done."

Joyce encouraged Lisa to move forward and see what happened, and said, "Maybe he will be better when you move."

Lisa thought, *IF she moved*. She decided not to mention this little tidbit to Derek. Derek had previously told Lisa that his children only called when they needed something; however, Derek no longer answered Lisa's phone call because he was always talking to his son. He and his son had become best friends in a matter of two weeks.

Lisa knew it wasn't Derek's son he was talking to, but Derek would make it a point to call Lisa insecure and jealous. He was punishing Lisa. Hey, he was a minister in the church, and his motto was, "I don't mess over people; they mess over me." HA! This dude was a joke.

Lisa made the first move as always and contacted Derek. She said, "Derek, we used to talk multiple times per day, and now we barely talk."

Derek yelled, "I'm talking to my son and you aren't more important than him! My son will come before you any day!"

OUCH! That was the real Derek. It stung, but he was honest.

Lisa was embarrassed, hurt, and shaken. She called Richard, who had already been married and divorced twice, and said, "Hi, Richard. I need to talk. Derek is evil. I haven't seen the fullness of his evil, but this boy is evil as hell."

Richard asked, "How so?"

Lisa caught Richard up to speed. Richard said, "Ouch. He's an asshole. I feel sorry for you because he married you for nothing. He married you to mistreat you, because there is no reason to be that angry over that incident. If he's that angry over something so minute, imagine how angry he will be over a major issue."

Lisa continued, "I'm happy I haven't moved with him because I couldn't live with this tension. I see why his ex-wife cheated on him. He's evil."

Richard and Lisa laughed. Richard suggested Lisa keep her eyes open because from a man's point of view, Derek was a bitch. Lisa was startled. Richard said, "This type of temper tantrum is a bitch move. I'm not calling women bitches, but Derek sounds like the type of guy who wants everything to go his way, and when it doesn't, he throws a tantrum. I just wished you had dated him longer than three months. Then you would have seen this ugly side and not married him. You are sharp, and I would guess he wanted to get married before he reared his ugly head. Just be careful."

Derek called Lisa and talked like there had been no tension or yelling. He never even apologized. Lisa texted Joyce, saying, 'This dude is like Dr. Jekyll and Mr. Hyde." His mood swings came and went faster than a pregnant woman. Everything changed after saying, "I do." Derek told Lisa he was angry as a child because he was rejected by his parents, which led to his competitive behavior. He said, "I had to win at everything, and that way I was accepted."

Derek believed he had outgrown that competitive nature and need for acceptance, but he hadn't. Lisa could hear it in his voice. Derek had become equally as competitive with Lisa. BM (before marriage) he was supportive; AM (after marriage), Derek was extremely competitive. Every dream Lisa shared with Derek, he would one-up her. If Lisa said she wanted to write books, so did Derek. If Lisa said one person asked her to pray with them, Derek would say two people asked him to pray with them.

A couple more weeks passed, and they were no longer talking as much. Their conversation was more "hi and bye." It was just polite banter. Derek acted as if he was doing Lisa a favor. Again, those mood swings were real. He was up and down. Lisa had been single so long and didn't know what to do with Derek's roller coaster of emotions. Derek had this uncanny way of bouncing back and reeling Lisa in with talking, texting, and joking. He was even fun on social media.

Chapter Nine

He Is a Demon

It was fun while it lasted. Suddenly, communication and activities ceased again. Derek would reel Lisa in, and throw her back out to sea. This type of behavior pissed her off. She was angrier at herself for marrying a fool. Derek was the chief of game playing. Lisa began crying uncontrollably, and screamed into the air, "You have gone and done it now! You thought you had married up because he's a self-professed Christian. God, what have I done? I have made a mistake. He seduced me with words, but his actions aren't lined up with his words. He seduced me with words, but he isn't the man he pretended to be."

Lisa deactivated her Facebook page because she didn't want to see or hear anything from this jive sucker. Lisa told her coworker, Linda, "Derek is demonic. You hear what I say? He's a demon in the flesh."

Linda laughed and stated, "Girl, a Christian can't have a demon."

Lisa said, "Maybe Derek isn't a Christian, and he's one of Satan's employees disguised as a minister. Heck, when I went to church with him, the entire atmosphere was cold." She shuddered and said, "I want out of this living hell. I feel it deep in the pit of my stomach that Derek acted impulsively too and wants out as well."

Linda stated, "I just think y'all are too far apart."

Lisa disagreed. "Something isn't right. How the hell do you go from talking ten times per day to one or sometimes none? There is no justification for that. That J. J. Walker-looking sucker is playing games."

Linda fell over with laughter, which made Lisa laugh too. Lisa went into the marriage with right intentions, but Derek's intentions were unclear. Lisa asked Derek why he was playing so many games and he cursed her out. He still didn't answer her question. Besides, Derek "didn't curse." Lisa didn't dare confront him because he would call her a liar. She heard the expletives. In his mind, he was perfect and one of the disciples, or maybe he was kin to Peter before Christ.

Lisa had a sinking feeling Derek was trying to see if she really loved him. He was administering these painful tests in order to test her loyalty. Derek was playing awful mind games in order to see how much Lisa loved him. His goal was to get her to kiss his assets and chase him as proof that she loved him. Lisa heard Derek loud and clear when he said, "Ain't nobody gone treat me like my ex-wife."

Lisa could tell Derek wasn't over his ex-wife and was still holding on to the pain he experienced during their marriage. After his first failed marriage, Derek became the predator. He needed full control and began exercising full control by playing mind games. Derek would talk, text, and disappear for days without responding. He would resurface like nothing happened and dared Lisa to question his behavior. It happened over and over again. Lisa started feeling like she was going crazy.

Guess what? All of this dysfunction occurred within six weeks of being married. Whenever Derek and Lisa talked, it was usually about his friends and their jacked-up relationships.

Derek and Lisa no longer spoke about themselves. They had settled into an uncomfortable routine. He complimented women at work, on television, and church, but *never* complimented Lisa. He talked about his ex-wife almost every day. Lisa was tired of hearing about all of the "things" he did for his first wife, and that she didn't appreciate it. Lisa was hoping Derek would go back and find his ex-wife, because he was still married to her in the spirit.

A few more weeks went by, and Derek asked Lisa, "Do you trust me?"

Without hesitating, Lisa answered, "No, I don't trust you." Lisa knew Derek was livid, but those words ended the already failed marriage. Derek exited the marriage on March 1. He wasn't happy two weeks after being married, and Lisa's admission gave him the fuel to become a tyrant for the duration of the marriage.

Derek asked, "Why did you marry me?"

Lisa didn't verbalize an answer. In her head, she felt as though she married Derek because she had finally made the commitment to be with someone regardless of the storm. She believed they shared similar goals, visions, dreams, and a love for Christ. The union hadn't manifested the way Lisa envisioned it in her head. She really believed two believers would walk it out together. Unfortunately, how can two walk together unless they agree?

CHAPTER TEN

THE VERBAL ABUSE

Lisa hoped the ground would open up and swallow her whole. Derek's verbal aggression was intolerable. He spoke to her in a condescending tone and manner with every opportunity. Derek was determined to make Lisa pay. Lisa apologized over and over again. It didn't matter. Derek never acknowledged or recognized that his actions and behavior contributed to Lisa's distrust of him.

Derek yelled, "You ruined this for me since day one when you got mad 'cause we stayed at my aunt's house! You ruined this marriage for me. It's no longer fun. I don't love you anyway!" There it was. Derek spoke what Lisa had known all along. Plus, Derek had been holding a grudge. He called Lisa at least three times per week to let her know she wasn't the woman she told him she was.

Despite Derek's verbal abuse, Lisa chose to ignore and forgive him. She told him she would like to work things out no matter how difficult. She was hurt, lonely, and confused. Lisa listened to the church women who encouraged her to pray for her husband and pray for her marriage. They encouraged Lisa to fight for her marriage. They told her to fast and pray for her husband. She prayed and fasted, and the demon in Derek grew stronger. Lisa took another approach and commenced to kissing Derek's "assets."

Lisa sounded like a pathetic human being who was practically begging a man to love her. She recognized she was pathetic and desperate, but she couldn't stop herself. Apparently, this was what women had to do in order to stay married. She had to treat her husband like he was sitting next to God and Jesus.

Lisa couldn't do anything to salvage this marriage. She tried everything in order to get in Derek's good graces. It didn't work. Derek punished Lisa with his words. He had a comeback to thwart every apology, and had found someone to validate his viewpoint. He called in order to taunt her.

Derek was so excited. He said, "I watched Bishop T. D. Jakes, and he said if a couple doesn't have trust, they don't have anything. We don't have anything."

Lisa said, "Trust has to be earned, and when behaviors change drastically, trust goes."

"If you knew your place, you wouldn't be so foolish. The Bible instructs a wife how to act," preached Derek. Lisa asked for a supporting Scripture. Derek was silent.

Lisa quoted, "In the same way, you husbands must give honor to your wives. Treat your wife with understanding as you live together. She may be weaker than you are, but she is your equal partner in God's gift of new life. Treat her as you should so your prayers won't be hindered" (1 Peter 3:7).

Derek sneered, "I've never heard that Scripture. You made that up." He wouldn't acknowledge that he had been strategically ignoring Lisa for weeks. She had had enough. She suggested they get an annulment or file for divorce, because clearly that one sentence in Bishop Jakes' sermon had confirmed Derek.

Lisa sought godly counsel. She told them she could have lied or beat around the bush, but she said what she felt. Heck, Derek became rigid right after their vows.

Rosalyn said, "You can't be honest with a man. They are fragile."

Lisa said, "That ninja isn't fragile. The ninja is meaner than a rattlesnake." Lisa never told them that Derek confessed that he didn't love her; nor did she tell them he cursed at her or called her nasty names. She was too embarrassed to tell anyone she had married the Ike Turner of verbal abuse. Derek wounded Lisa with his tongue. With that same tongue he flattered everyone around him.

Joyce said, "You have apologized and that is all you can do. Don't chase him. He already told his family he wasn't happy with you. If he can't accept your apology, he's done anyway. He just needed an excuse."

Ouch! Lisa knew Joyce was right. Derek wanted out, but he was going to make Lisa pay for stripping him of his "happiness."

It's funny. Although Lisa suggested a divorce, Derek didn't agree. She thought maybe there was hope. A week or two went by and Derek had transformed into this happy-go-lucky husband. Lisa knew neither she nor Jesus was at the center of his joy. She wondered who or what contributed to his happiness.

Chapter Eleven

His New Coworker

A new female began working with Derek, and that relationship brought him so much joy. He talked about his coworker every day, and how much she depended upon him. Lisa could hear joy in Derek's voice. He said, "Tonya moved here and doesn't have family, so I invited her to church. She's always asking me for advice. Plus, neither one of us likes the boss."

Lisa encouraged Derek to be careful, because most affairs start in the workplace. He was so happy that her comment didn't faze him. Derek typically called Lisa insecure when she spoke her truth. Lisa and Linda would share laughs about Derek's work wife.

Lisa said, "Girl, Derek is happy, and he has a crush on his new coworker."

Linda laughed and said, "Girl, you are stupid. Men do need to feel needed, and he probably feels good that she's dependent upon him."

Lisa said, "Yep. Derek likes the feeling of newness. He's the type that likes the new-car smell. It won't be long before Derek finds a way of escape."

Linda asked, "How can you be so sure?"

Lisa replied, "My gut is telling me that this man has one leg in and one leg out of the marriage. The thrill is gone for him. The new-car smell has gone for him. He's fascinated with his work wife."

Lisa began looking for divorce attorneys. Derek was in such a good mood lately because he was able to talk about Tonya. His entire conversation was Tonya this and Tonya that. He was in a state of euphoria, on cloud nine, and invited Lisa to spend the week with him.

Lisa told Joyce she was going to visit Derek. Joyce said, "Take some anointing oil and anoint everything in his house, including his shoes, clothes, doorposts, and get those demonic attachments out of him and his home."

Lisa laughed and said, "Duly noted."

She packed and made the drive to Texas. Derek and Lisa laughed and talked. Of course, Derek talked about Tonya as well. Tonya had temporarily replaced his ex-wife. He complained that Tonya had two children and their fathers weren't helping her. Derek couldn't understand the type of man who would neglect his family.

Lisa thought inwardly, *Is Derek listening to himself? Probably not, because he was so prideful and didn't believe he did anything wrong.* Lisa asked Derek if he would go and get her something to eat. While he was gone, Lisa prayed and anointed Derek's shoes, underwear, clothes, bed, sofa, walls, and doorknobs. "God, I'm in this; what will You have me to do? I can't make him love me."

Outside of sex, Lisa and Derek had nothing. They didn't read or study the Bible. Derek had his Bible open on the coffee table. Lisa watched him read a verse or two, and he was done. He had that self-satisfying look, as though he just read heaven down to earth. She realized that was the reason he wasn't well versed in Scripture. He only knew the popular verses that saints and sinners knew. It was obvious to Lisa that Derek had a public and private persona.

Lisa was sitting on the sofa doing homework while Derek was on the other sofa watching television. Neither one of them kept food in their homes. Lisa had a term paper due and couldn't take a break. She asked Derek if he would grab them some food. He continued watching television and said, "I don't like moving my car when I'm off work."

Lisa shook her head and mumbled, "Asshole." It aggravated him to go and get his "wife" something to eat.

Derek's cell phone rang shortly afterwards, and he answered in a half a second. Mind you, he had been strategically ignoring Lisa's calls and texts. Lisa smiled because he used to answer the phone that quickly for her.

Derek whispered, "It's Tonya; she needs to talk." After several hours of pleading for food, Derek finally left in order to get her some. He left while talking to Tonya and reentered the home talking to her as well.

CHAPTER TWELVE

FEELING REJECTED

L isa smiled. This ninja isn't "the man" he claimed to be either. Derek loved calling her "a fake-ass Christian." He called her a fake Christian because he was one too. Lisa was polite, but she was aware that this farce of a marriage would be over soon.

Lisa mulled over if she should mention her concern to Derek. What the heck? She wasn't about to continue in bondage. She said, "Derek, Tonya is a lucky girl. She can call a married man who responds to her faster than he does his wife." Derek, lacking compassion, again called Lisa insecure and jealous. Any wise man could see that this behavior was disrespectful.

When Lisa looked into Derek's eyes, they were cold and didn't display any emotion. He had the characteristics of a sociopath. He was constantly testing Lisa's loyalty and trust. He used Facebook as his desktop, left his page open, and headed for the shower. A voice whispered, *He wants to see if you are going to look on his page*. Lisa had no intentions on looking; nor did she move, but continued doing her homework.

After Derek got out of the shower, he came straight to the living room. He looked shocked because Lisa was in the same spot, covered in papers. She had a thirty-page paper due by midnight and didn't have time to stalk his Facebook page.

Lisa knew when you went looking for something, you would find it.

Although Lisa never searched Derek's page, he falsely accused her of doing so. He accused her of going on his ex-wife's and ex-girlfriend's pages. This was so sad because he spent more time trying to discredit her. He loved to falsely accuse her of everything, more specifically of being insecure and manipulative. Unbeknownst to Lisa, she provided Derek with the ammunition to continuously call her insecure.

Lisa has never had a big booty. Everyone in the family teased her because of her genetic makeup. They would say she had a flat bottom like her godmother. This always made her laugh because it was funny. She would joke with Derek just as she has done her family and friends. She joked about getting butt implants and doing squats in order to get a more pronounced booty.

Derek yelled, "You are insecure! You're jealous of my ex-girlfriend because she has a big booty. You stalked her page."

Lisa sat stunned. Derek had never mentioned his ex-girl-friend's name, so how could she go on her page? She wasn't jealous, and calmly said, "Derek, my family and I have joked about my flat buttocks for years. Whenever I'm around them we joke about me getting a big booty. This has been a joke within my family and friends for more than twenty years, but you have reduced it to an insecurity and jealousy. Honey, all of my friends have better bodies and are prettier than me and your ex-girlfriend combined. If I can hang around them, I can't be insecure because they exemplify beauty and body."

Lisa realized that Derek was building a good case for his departure. He was painting Lisa as some insecure psycho so that he could tell everyone he met another "broken" woman.

Derek had to have a story, and he had to be the victim. Derek had been in and out of bed with multiple women, even women in his church. However, he loved to declare women as broken. Derek was also broken and damaged.

Lisa was so happy she had friends who were supportive. Joyce and Debra had been Lisa's friends since the first grade. She could be vulnerable with them. She told Joyce and Debra that Derek was mean and surly.

Joyce stated, "I believe you. Any husband unwilling to forgive his wife isn't a good husband. He doesn't want to be bothered."

Debra said, "I should have said something before you married him. My boyfriend told me that he got a sense that Derek was crazy anyway. I looked at him before the ceremony and told my boo that he does look crazy. He didn't look like he was into you anyway. There is something shady about him and it's best he goes before he disrupts your life any further."

Lisa wanted a divorce and had discussed it earlier. Derek was indecisive. He wanted out, but then he wanted in. Lisa wanted to work on the marriage because it was heart wrenching to have waited seven years for a mate and have it end within two months. She listened to all of the Christian women who said, "Pray for your husband." She continued praying and believing that God's will would be done for the marriage.

When things were good, Derek would open up about some of his goals. One of his goals was to get a college degree. He felt unfulfilled because both his ex-wife and current wife had completed graduate and postgraduate degrees. Derek was interested in going back to school. Lisa encouraged him to apply for financial aid and go. She was supportive of his dream.

Derek reminded her again, "I put my first wife through school, and now it's my time."

Lisa smiled, "It's never too late."

Lisa and Derek were civil. Derek was excited and began his journey to enroll in college. But Lisa noticed Derek's happiness was situational. The only thing they had in common was they both had horrible bosses. It was a shame they had to find something in common just to have a conversation. Most of their conversation centered around work.

Lisa was tired of her supervisor's lies and psychosis. She tolerated her supervisor because she understood mental illness. Derek, on the other hand, hated his supervisor. He didn't like his boss to say anything to him. Lisa would encourage Derek to try and respect his boss's position. She told him her boss was a white supremacist and a witch, but she still hadn't cursed, yelled, or disrespected her.

Did Lisa want to smack that witch? Yes! However, she showed restraint in the workplace. Lord knows, white people love to stereotype us as "angry black women." She wasn't going to give that heifer the opportunity to spread that lie and played the game that most black women had to play. She had to grin and bear it, but she fussed and cussed at home.

Lisa understood how difficult it was for Derek because he wanted to be promoted so badly. Plus, he wanted to be accepted by his coworkers. She prayed with him and tried to give him strategy on how to deal with his boss.

Derek said, "He pretends to be a Christian, but he ain't no Christian. He's two-faced."

Lisa was thinking, *This is the pot calling the kettle two-faced,* but she wouldn't dare verbalize her thoughts. She would often shake her head because Derek was always the victim, even in the workplace. She kept asking God what it was about Derek. She knew he was full of pride, but she was missing something. There were underlying mental health issues.

Lisa calmly said, "Derek, you have a prideful spirit. No one can say anything to you and you don't listen."

Well, that ticked Derek off. He told her she was negative and she didn't have his back, and abruptly hung up. Lisa looked at her phone and thought, *This guy is a complete idiot.* She whispered, "I'm sorry God, but this man has a self-destructive spirit. Who ordained him a minister? He has no insight or wisdom, only pride."

Lisa decided to give Derek some space. One week later, Derek expressed his anger and proudly let Lisa know, "At least Tonya understands me. Samuel is picking on her too." He said, "Tonya is new, and he hasn't given her a chance, which shows he isn't worthy to be a supervisor."

Lisa agreed. "I believe you are being treated unfairly; however, your response is unbecoming of a man of God." Derek eventually mellowed out, but he continued complaining about his supervisor's ill treatment of him and Tonya.

Weeks went by and the dynamics had changed in Derek's workplace. One day, Samuel took Tonya to lunch, and Derek was seething. Derek called Lisa and he was fuming. Lisa asked, "Why are you so angry?"

Derek replied, "Samuel took Tonya to lunch, and now she's all up in his face. She hasn't even spoken to me today." While Lisa was on the phone with Derek, he kept saying, "Look at Tonya, laughing all up in Samuel's face!"

Lisa said, "Oh dear, Tonya has just broken your heart by laughing and talking to the enemy."

Derek wasn't pleased and hung up the phone. Lisa laughed. She thought about Derek's story and his behavior. Derek was rejected by Tonya. Lisa gasped. Derek was dealing with rejection. She reflected on past conversations. Derek clung to women because he never had his mother's love. It all made sense. His three closest friends were women. He only talked to women at church and work. He felt some sort of attraction to his female coworker.

He had only one male friend, and Lisa found that strange. He was so withdrawn. It was almost as if he was hiding from people. Lisa presumed Derek was hiding that wounded and hurt little boy on the inside. He presented himself as this good man who did no wrong, a conversationalist, and a great listener. Everyone else saw Derek's representative. Lisa saw Derek. Derek had never acknowledged that he was in pain after being rejected by his parents. He was sent to live with his aunt and uncle when he was ten years old.

Derek often talked about how he never understood why his parents gave him away but kept his two younger siblings. He was dealing with the ultimate rejection from his parents. Your foundation can make you or break you. Lisa was finally able to put a name to Derek's anger. He was so angry, but he hid it well.

Lisa was a scapegoat. People outside of his bubble probably never saw this side of him. Derek was a case study for Lisa. She was intrigued. Lisa also noticed some narcissistic characteristics. This was fascinating. How did she end up with a narcissist? A lot of people have married spouses with an undiagnosed mental illness. The problems are deeper than what was on the surface.

In Lisa's line of work, she talked to a lot of people. Oftentimes, her Facebook posts were a compilation of her conversations with other people. All of Lisa and Derek's close friends were having relationship problems, and Lisa would take portions of their conversations and post them (with their permission). Mind you, Lisa was doing this before ever meeting Derek. Plus, Lisa had studied Marriage and Family Therapy in graduate school.

Lisa never had anyone complain about her posts until Derek. In his mind, every post was about him. Lisa created a status about marriage not being honored like it used to and how people were doing these drive-by marriages. It appeared everyone wanted to "Keep Up with The Kardashians" twenty-four hours and done.

Derek called Lisa in a rage, "You're talking about me and putting our business on Facebook. My uncle called me and asked if we were having problems because of your posts."

Lisa rolled her eyes, because she hadn't had any issues on Facebook until she married Derek. Every post was watched by one of his relatives, and Derek would call, yelling and screaming. Some of Lisa's posts about marriage were from her graduate program. She wasn't prepared for this level of scrutiny. All of this voyeuristic behavior was getting on her nerves, especially Derek. She was beginning to despise him. She was the only one being encouraged to change.

Lisa said, "The posts were partially about us, but it was also about other people."

Derek seethed, "You're a liar and a manipulator. I saw another post I didn't like, but I didn't say anything. I told you I was loyal, and people are always hurting me first." Derek went off on a tangent.

Lisa was wondering who Derek was talking to, because he was clearly not talking to her. It was as if he was taking his frustration out on her. It seemed like Derek was saying everything to Lisa that he wanted to say to other women but didn't get the opportunity. He accused her of things she had no knowledge of. He was angry at someone else, and Lisa was getting the brunt of that anger. He dumped all of his rage onto her, and she started becoming ill after talking to him. Her head and stomach hurt every time she heard his voice, and she would become nauseous.

Every time she talked to Derek, she was walking on eggshells. She was trying to show love to an unlovable husband. Lisa had learned a soft answer turns away wrath, but not Derek's. He loved to argue, but she wouldn't entertain that foolery. He blamed her for all of the problems within the marriage.

Lisa was tired mentally, emotionally, and spiritually. Derek was constantly training her to focus on his feelings, never mind hers. She began blaming herself. This debacle of a marriage was draining. Nevertheless, Lisa was still willing to try. God softened Pharoah's heart; maybe there was hope for Derek.

CHAPTER THIRTEEN

FOR BETTER OR WORSE

For better or for worse. The worst came first. It was going to get better. It had to. Lisa sought God and godly counsel. "Plans fail for lack of counsel, but with many advisers they succeed" (Proverbs 15:22). Lisa opened up to her prayer group. It was raw and honest, but painful. She told them, "I could have married a man who believed in God and Jesus but doesn't go to church and got better results than with Nabal."

Ms. Martin look confused. "I thought your husband's name was Derek."

"It is, but I call him Nabal. Nabal means fool." They say you attract what you are. Lisa must be a major fool, because she definitely married one.

Evangelists Thomas and Clark prayed with Lisa. Evangelist Clark was more of a proponent for marriage. She and her husband had divorced and remarried. Evangelist Clark called Lisa daily and encouraged her to pray for her husband because God had shown her that he wasn't delivered. Evangelist Clark said, "Derek wants to be married on his terms, not God's terms, but continue to pray for him."

In the back of Lisa's mind, she knew she wasn't willing to war for Derek's soul. She told Evangelist Clark that she would pray that he treated his next wife better because he was already in a relationship. Evangelist Clark asked, "How do you know that?"

Lisa replied, "He has a problem with lust, and his flesh wants what it wants; therefore, he can't be single."

Lisa took heed to the advice from the women of God and prayed for Derek. She fasted and prayed and fasted and prayed. Lisa and Derek ended up on good terms for a little while. Lisa was leery because she experienced bouts of nausea whenever she talked to Derek. The sound of Derek's voice made her ill.

Lisa actually smiled at the thought of the women who "cheated" on him or "dogged" him out. They had the courage to give back what he was dishing out. Lisa could understand why his ex-wife and previous girlfriends found comfort in the arms of other men. She had only been with Derek for a total of three months dating and two months married, and this had been her worst relationship to date.

Lisa admired Derek because he was able to be a different person to those who mattered or those he was trying to impress. The Derek behind closed doors was ten different people. Lisa walked around in a daze. She had given up a peaceful and powerful single life for a miserable marriage.

Derek wasn't very attentive, nurturing, or loving. He wasn't romantic; nor did he show any emotions. He lacked empathy. Derek was like a brick wall. He was protecting himself from being hurt ever again. His first wife hurt him, and he was determined that he would never hurt again. Hurt people, hurt people. Derek was projecting his hurt onto Lisa.

Derek had everyone else thinking that he was over his ex-wife, but he wasn't. He was still connected to the affair she had in the home they built. The main reason Lisa knew Derek wasn't over his ex-wife was because he refused to love again.

He was doing marriage on his terms this time around. He was in the driver's seat and Lisa was in the backseat.

Derek was so attached to his ex-wife that he became angry that she wasn't answering his call. He was so insensitive. He actually called Lisa in order to vent. Lisa laughed inwardly and couldn't help herself. She stated, "You haven't called your current wife all day, and the only reason you called was to vent about your ex-wife not answering your phone calls. Who does that?"

Derek yelled, "You are just pathetic! You're too insecure and manipulative. I don't know why I called you with your stupid self."

Lisa responded, "Okay. I'm not the one obsessed with my ex. Clearly, she controls you because you're angry that she hasn't answered her ex-husband's phone call. Her *ex-husband*. You do realize she isn't married to you, right?"

Derek said, "We have a child together and I was calling for him."

Lisa said, "So, your twenty-year-old son has a problem with his mother regarding her money and you're going to make her spend her money on y'all son."

Derek spoke through clenched teeth, "She knows I don't play."

Lisa said, "Your child vented to you about his disappointment concerning a matter, but he also told you the issue would be resolved. However, you're still trying to control your ex-wife and her money, and according to you she still wants you, so you're playing a game." Lisa thought about the irony.

While she was calling Derek, he was calling his ex-wife. This reminded her of a scene from the movie, *My Best Friend's Wedding*. Julia Roberts's character was chasing Dermot

Mulroney's character, but he was chasing the woman he truly loved, which was Cameron Diaz's character. Folks judging Lisa and calling her an overthinker. *Ha!* The proof was in the pudding.

Lisa was two seconds from telling Derek to remarry his ex-wife because she was tired of living the song by The O'Jays, "Your body's here with me, but your mind and heart are on the other side of town; you're messing me around."

Derek called Lisa stupid in addition to other colorful names. Lisa said, "You're divorced but still expect your ex-wife to jump for you. That's stupid." Derek had the nerve to say she was probably laid up with some man. Lisa asked, "How long ago did you say you were divorced?" Derek didn't respond. "If I recall, you have been divorced for ten years. If she's laid up with a man, she's well within her rights."

Derek said, "She was dating as soon as we got a divorce. I told her she better not have all of those different men around my children."

Lisa felt like she was a part of a social experiment. "I never told my ex anything about dating. I always introduced myself to the women and told them that my children should respect them, and if it became problematic, feel free to contact me. I never tried to control who their dad dated. He was no longer my problem." Of course, Derek wasn't pleased with Lisa's response, and hung up in Lisa's face again.

Lisa's supporters still encouraged her to pray for Derek's deliverance. She felt like he had to want deliverance. Heck, Derek was so prideful. Lisa never heard him ask for forgiveness nor repent. Derek probably didn't think he needed deliverance from anything. He didn't see anything wrong with his behavior. When he hung up in Lisa's face, yelled, and called her names, he believed in his heart that she deserved to be treated that way.

Nevertheless, Lisa prayed and fasted, fasted and prayed. she told Derek that she had just concluded a fast. He said, "You're supposed to tell your husband that you're fasting."

Lisa stated, "We aren't in the same house, so I didn't think about it."

Derek said, "That's very disrespectful. You aren't submissive. I asked you to take the weave out of your hair, and you wouldn't; now you're fasting without telling me."

Lisa responded, "You have a warped definition of submission. I told you I would eventually remove the weave, but right now it isn't convenient."

Derek stated, "I like to run my fingers through a woman's hair and feel her scalp."

Lisa stated, "Like I said, I'll take the weave out eventually, or maybe not." She thought to herself, *Controlling demon.*

She asked Derek to start praying and reading the Word like they used to. Derek snapped, "I was reading the Word before I met you. I don't need to read the Word with you. You act like I need you to study the Word."

Lisa stated, "You didn't have a problem reading and praying when we were dating." She could see the self-satisfying smug on his face. Derek had this indescribable look on his face when he felt like he wounded her. He looked as if he had won the lottery or something. It was a look like, *I put you in your place* kind of look*, and I don't have to do anything you ask.* He was letting Lisa know she wasn't the boss of him.

She recognized her error. She was supposed to let Derek suggest studying and praying. Derek loathed Lisa making any suggestions or decisions. She would often joke about being married to Mister (from *The Color Purple*). The marriage was awful and there was no coming back.

Lisa spent time praying for herself and her husband. She also prayed about her stupidity, realizing she was one dumb chick. A smart woman wouldn't have married Derek. Clearly, Lisa felt dumb as hell. She prayed for God to deliver Derek from his pain. He wasn't a complete butthole, but he was a butthole in pain. Derek was a charming person. Women loved talking to him because he could hold a conversation. Behind all of that charm was an unhealed little boy masquerading as a man.

CHAPTER FOURTEEN

A SNAKE IN THE HOUSE

Women secretly hope their mates or husbands will engage them in conversation, like Lisa hoped about Derek. Derek was good to external women; however, behind closed doors he was like the husbands these women were complaining about. Derek never complimented Lisa; he complimented everyone except her. Every woman wants to hear a kind word from their spouse or significant other occasionally.

The more Lisa prayed, the worse Derek's behavior became. Lisa became tired of church women telling her to pray for her husband and to fight for her marriage. The more Lisa fought for her marriage, the more Derek grew colder and colder. His words were like venom. Venom attacks the neurotoxins in the brain, shutting down nerve function and arresting muscle movements. Lisa became immobile after speaking with Derek. Her brain and muscles would temporarily shut down.

Lisa saw a python type spirit on Derek. She began having nightmares about snakes trying to squeeze her to death. Lisa's face was breaking out, she wasn't sleeping, and she began losing weight. She was tired. Derek began feeling bad because people at his church were asking when Lisa would arrive. Derek said, "I don't like people in my business."

Lisa thought to herself how much of a liar Derek was. He told his business to the people at church, work, and his circle of friends. He liked to tell his version and not the whole truth.

Lisa was looking for jobs in Arlington, but nothing came through. Derek told Lisa he sowed a $10 faith seed with hopes she could find a job. She looked at Derek but inwardly thought, *No, not another cheap man. Ugh. Why God? Why? Why do I attract stingy men?*

Derek had introduced Lisa to one of his confidantes, Ms. Williams. Lisa called her and asked if she could help her find a job. Ms. Williams was gracious. She encouraged Lisa to move without a job. Lisa didn't want to tell Ms. Williams that she wasn't about to move without a job.

A few weeks had gone by when Ms. Williams contacted Lisa about the move to Arlington. They were on that downward cycle yet again. Lisa could have lied, but she decided not to. Lisa said, "Ms. Williams, Derek and I are contemplating divorce. As a matter of fact, it will be a matter of time."

Ms. Williams said, "Sorry to hear that. Let me pray with you." Ms. Williams called Derek with her concern. Derek called Lisa and let her have it.

Derek suddenly became a prophet (wink, wink). He prophesied these words, "The Lord has shown me that you're talking about me to too many people and you need to shut up. SHUT UP. SHUT UP. Do you hear and understand me? I said SHUT UP and SHUT UP NOW."

Lisa said, "So, you can talk to everyone about what's going on, but I can't. Oh, I forgot. You have to be the victim and your story is the only version people get."

Derek began calling Lisa manipulative amongst other things. Lisa said, "I am trying to maintain a level of peace, but I didn't feel like lying or avoiding Ms. Williams's inquiry."

Derek said, "You're a fake Christian."

Lisa was laughing and crying. She was crying because she was reaping everything she had ever sown, from stealing a piece of bubble gum to smoking her grandmother's cigarettes when she was only twelve years old. She was living in her own *Lifetime* movie.

Derek never apologized, but called like nothing happened. He suggested they seek marital counseling with his pastor. They picked the date and time for Lisa to call in. She conceded, "Okay, whatever you want to do." She was going along to get along. She felt defeated. It was all about Derek.

Lisa and Derek communicated cordially, but it always ended in an argument. Derek was always the instigator. He loved confrontations and arguments. Lisa wrote Derek's pastor and first lady and suggested they get him some help before he destroyed another woman's life. Derek was angry and said, "My pastor ain't my daddy, and he can't tell me what to do. I don't have to listen to him."

Lisa said, "I know, and that's why you're completely lost. You don't listen to anyone. Your pastor, like me, must not be sensitive to the Holy Spirit because he has a snake on his ministerial team, and I have one in my bed. Your undelivered, unholy, and self-righteous behind is praying over people and transferring your demonic spirits unto innocent people."

Lisa's cousin told her to pray because Derek did sound like a man who had a demonic spirit. Lisa said, "I don't feel like Derek is worth the fight."

Monica said, "You're his rib and you have to protect his inner parts. You have to pray for him because you're his wife."

Lisa said, "I don't have the energy to war for Derek. This demon has to be cast out, and I don't have the strength to do it. I'm sorry. You can pray for his deliverance. It's too much."

Joyce called to see if things were progressing. She was on her second marriage; however, she and her husband had a special union. They loved each other, and anyone who looked at them knew they loved each other to the core.

Lisa said, "I'm tired of the name-calling, but no one would believe me because he's the "good minister.""

Joyce said, "I believe you. After you told me he wouldn't forgive you, that is a huge sign of a stubborn person. Start recording y'all phone calls, and if y'all go to court, get him on grounds of verbal abuse."

Lisa said, "Girl, you know I'm technologically challenged. I only know how to talk and text. I am getting tired of begging and chasing a man. That isn't my job to chase my husband. I'm literally begging this man to stay married, and his ego is growing in the process."

Joyce was slightly agitated, "Don't keep apologizing to him. Give me his number, and I'll call and tell him how silly he is."

They both laughed. Lisa said, "No. Thanks for the support, because he will probably curse at you, and that will set your husband off."

Joyce said, "Are you sure that you and Jacob aren't supposed to be together?"

Lisa said, "What the hell does Jacob have to do with this?"

Joyce said, "He has followed you to Oklahoma."

Lisa said, "I left Jacob in 1995 and it's 2012. I haven't flirted, prayed, or consulted God for restoration. Besides, that joker hasn't improved financially, mentally, or spiritually, and I won't let him destroy what I've worked hard to accomplish."

Joyce said, "I'm just making sure, because Derek isn't the one."

Lisa replied, "Neither is Jacob. I'm not going backwards. Jacob probably wishes he could get me back. That's scary, because he and Derek are similar. Jacob moved to Oklahoma and lives close to me. Derek lives around the corner from his ex-wife. Who would do that except unstable people?"

Both of them were probably fantasizing about woulda, shoulda, coulda. Lisa would rather be a lesbian than get back with Jacob. Lisa *was* contemplating being a lesbian after being married to Derek.

Derek had become extremely pleasant. It never failed. Every time Lisa was planning to end the marriage, he reeled her back in with his charm. She didn't realize this was the calm before the storm. Derek had begun discussing the type of house they would purchase, the neighborhood, the tile, and décor. They began FaceTiming each other. Derek presented with humanlike qualities. It was frightening. Lisa couldn't fully enjoy this new Derek because his behavior was unpredictable.

Things were going a lot better until Lisa needed a root canal. She was referred to a specialist who wanted to perform the root canal immediately because the infection had gotten worse. The pain was so excruciating, she couldn't think. She was completing the paperwork for the insurance, but couldn't remember Derek's date of birth. She texted him and told him she could remember the month and date, but not the year he was born. She needed the correct year.

Derek wouldn't answer but responded by calling Lisa childish. She explained that she was serious and couldn't remember the year he was born. Derek didn't respond to any more text messages. The front-desk clerk told Lisa not to worry about it because the dentist was ready for her. The dentist performed oral surgery and Lisa went back to the office under heavy pain meds. Derek called and Lisa could barely talk.

Derek snapped, "How much is the bill?" He never asked Lisa how she was doing.

Lisa replied, "Three hundred and eighty-seven dollars."

Derek said, "I'll send you half. Why did you go back to work?"

Lisa said, "You know I work for a witch and can't take off."

Derek was snapping at Lisa, but just as quickly he would speak politely to Tonya. Lisa heard laughter in the background. Derek said, "I'll check on you later." He hung up abruptly. He was so rude, and never called to check on her.

Lisa called Derek after her mouth healed and thanked him for checking on her and sending half of the money for the bill. Her sarcasm didn't go over very well. Derek called her childish, jealous, insecure, and stupid. Lisa rolled her eyes and thought, *This dude has a very limited vocabulary.* He used the same words over and over again.

Lisa noticed Derek began calling when he knew she wouldn't be available. She returned his calls, but he wouldn't answer. She called one Saturday morning and he was distracted. Lisa asked, "Derek, I thought we were starting over."

Derek snapped, "I'm texting my son and you don't come before him."

Lisa knew in her gut Derek was texting another woman. He wasn't this faithful character he portrayed. She said, "I'm going to drive to Arlington and settle this once and for all."

Derek threatened, "You better NOT come to my house unannounced."

Lisa mimicked, "We don't talk, don't come to your house, let's go to counseling, let's buy a house, let's start over, let's work on the marriage, you're stupid. I can't find a good woman. No one treats me right."

In his typical fashion, Derek hung up. This grown man loved to hang up abruptly, but Lisa was childish. She chuckled.

Mind you, Lisa had applied for several jobs in Arlington, TX. She was hired for a federal position but it meant a huge pay cut. Lisa told Derek she had a job offer but the pay was significantly less. She didn't trust him to help her financially. After all, he never paid half of Lisa's dentist bill.

Derek wasn't excited about Lisa's job. It angered him. After sharing the news with her prayer team, they encouraged Lisa to accept the job. Evangelist Clark said, "That is a federal job and you'll be able to transfer after a year. Look at the bright side; if the marriage fails, you'll have a steady job and can transfer to another city or state after your first year."

Lisa's prayer group wasn't listening. Lisa was slightly perturbed, "Derek told me not to come to his house so I'll have to find my own place."

Evangelist Clark said, "You never know how God works. God could be sending you to Arlington in order to minister to your husband."

Lisa didn't say a word. She continued being told not to give up on her marriage because God would hold her accountable. Everywhere Lisa turned there were sermons about what the wife should do in order to keep the husband happy. There were sermons after sermons, Facebook marriage ministries, and sermons that all catered to how the wife should treat her husband.

Lisa prayed, "God, I see why men treat their wives like dirt. All of the sermons are geared towards what a wife should do in order to keep the marriage together, but the husbands have no accountability. I should have stayed single. I was accountable for me." Lisa's thinking went into overdrive.

She began assessing all of their conversations. As long as everything was on Derek's terms, he was happy. He needed someone to agree with him and constantly make him feel good. Lisa was noncombative as the girlfriend, but Derek was a pleasant boyfriend. She tried to push him when they were dating because she wanted to see his angry side and how he handled conflict.

Derek was always even-tempered and responded with love before they were married. Although Lisa knew Derek was lying about all of his relationships, she listened. It took two people to cause a relationship to fail. According to Derek, he was perfect and everyone else was flawed.

This was a difficult decision because the federal position only paid $46,000. Derek earned $50,000, whereas she earned $80,000. Lisa weighed her options. She was doing well in Oklahoma, but this was a contract position without benefits. Lisa couldn't be dependent upon Derek. She wouldn't allow him to have bragging rights about building and supporting her. She wouldn't give him the satisfaction of bragging to his friend about giving her money, paying off credit cards, sending her to college, or paying her car note.

The only story he could share was Lisa was stupid, childish, insecure, jealous, manipulative, fake, crazy, and not the woman she said she was. Derek loved to create stories and he had the starring role. He was a male version of a diva. He had a strong support system of women too. They fed the monster.

Lisa contemplated about all of the times she attended church with Derek. He never said "Amen." He never clapped during the sermon. He sat there like it was his duty to come to church. In hindsight, Derek sat in church like he was doing God a favor.

Lisa thought about a previous conversation with him that caused her to fall over on the bed with laughter. Derek bragged about how he was praying over people and laying hands on them. They were being slain in the Spirit, according to him. He said his ex-wife called and told him she heard he was laying folks out at the altar. Lisa hollered. He was laying folks out, all right. Those demons were being transferred from him to them. A wolf praying and preying on God's sheep.

Derek's prayers were rehearsed. He said "Father God" over and over again. Father God and Father God and Father God and Father God. When Derek used to pray, Lisa would open her eyes and look up to heaven because she still couldn't understand how and who made him a minister. His prayers were only reaching the ceiling. Derek was mentally ill. The older he became, the worse his symptoms became. To an untrained eye, they would just excuse it as "That's just how Derek is."

Lisa knew the perfect person to call, Bonnie, a licensed professional counselor, and one of the smartest people she knew. Lisa informed Bonnie about Derek's behavior, especially how he accused her of doing things she wasn't doing. She told her everything from A to Z.

Without hesitating, Bonnie replied, "Derek has PPD (Paranoid Personality Disorder), which is a long-standing suspiciousness and generalized mistrust of others. When you told Derek you didn't trust him, he was already thinking it, and your truth confirmed it. He's paranoid. He would never have accepted your apology because he's guarded. He lives with the mentality that he will never find a good woman and all of the women he meets are broken. He never saw the real you. He judged you based off his past relationships. He just needed a reason to lash out at."

Lisa was amazed with Bonnie's assessment of Derek and said, "That is exactly what he said. He said he keeps meeting women who are broken."

Bonnie said, "He's the common denominator in all of these relationships. Clearly, he doesn't recognize his role in the demise of the relationships. I can assure you that you aren't the only one who he has called names. He just hides that side of him from other people. He's angry with you because y'all know mutual people. He has an image to maintain and you can threaten that image he has created. He has a lot of issues and folks are dismissing it and making him the victim. They are feeding into his mental illness, and that isn't helping. This disorder begins in childhood or adolescence."

Lisa said, "Go on, because I knew he was disturbed but not how sick he really is."

Bonnie inquired, "So you say he has four good friends; three females and one male, correct?"

Lisa replied, "Yes."

Bonnie continued, "They love him unconditionally. He hides himself from people and only socializes with people he believes can't see the real him. He talks and takes over the conversation in order to appear intelligent and confident, but if they really listen, they will hear his wounds and insecurity. He doesn't want people to know the real him, so he's safe with those four because they only know what he tells them. They probably don't challenge him."

Lisa asked, "Is that where the ugliness and anger comes from? He's very condescending, but he doesn't receive criticism very well. He hates being told or asked what to do. However, he can switch up in public or in front of people he's trying to impress, especially church members."

Bonnie continued, "PPD is common in men. How does Derek get along with people at work, church?"

Lisa said, "Derek doesn't hang out with people. He's antisocial. He will socialize with people if he can sell himself. He presents an image and he doesn't want it tarnished. He doesn't get along with his coworkers. He only seems to get along with women. He loves talking to and engaging women. I think that stems from his mother rejecting him."

Bonnie said, "Derek has all of the classic symptoms. He doesn't work well with others and that's why he isolates himself. He appears to be critical of you, but if you offend him, he's hypersensitive. More importantly, people with PPD lack forgiveness. They lack the ability to forgive."

Lisa said, "I knew it. He hasn't forgiven his mother, father, brothers, ex-wife, ex-girlfriends, me, or himself. He holds on to everything and carries it into the next relationship. It will take a patient woman to deal with him, and God forbid if she makes a mistake; he's going to destroy her self-esteem."

She thanked Bonnie for her insight, which she never doubted. However, Lisa wanted more information about this disorder because she had been accused of being insecure, crazy, and an overthinker.

Lisa worked with mental health professionals. She picked the brain of her esteemed colleague, Dr. Daniels, PsyD. Lisa brought Dr. Daniels up to speed and told him about Bonnie's assessment.

Dr. Daniels said, "You have been dealing with this and coming to work unbothered? To look at you, I wouldn't have guessed that you were going through anything."

Lisa said, "I cry enough at home when I'm alone. I can't allow the clients to see me broken down, busted, and disgusted."

Dr. Daniels said, "I have to agree with Bonnie. Paranoid Personality Disorder is one of a group of conditions called Cluster A personality disorders, which involves eccentric ways of thinking. This disorder begins early on and it appears more common in men. People with PPD are always on guard or believe people are constantly trying to harm or threaten them. They have unfounded beliefs and that can impair their relationships or prevent them from having close relationships with others. Most of their relationships are superficial. The relationships are on the surface and not too deep. People with PPD doubt commitment, loyalty, and always believe others are deceiving them. They hold grudges and are unforgiving. They criticize but don't like criticism."

Lisa was visibly shaken and said, "Dr. Daniels, Derek kept accusing me of not being the type of woman I said I was. One of my good friends even questioned my integrity by asking what type of woman I told him I was. I was offended by that question, I guess. He always told me I didn't love him, regardless of how many times I said it."

Dr. Daniels said, "He heard whatever he wanted to hear and drew his own conclusions. He probably compared you to every other woman he had ever dated. Three months isn't enough time to know everything about a person. He only knows a portion of who you are. Don't take it personally, because he has to create this image of you to make himself feel better. You have to remember, people with PPD are suspicious. When did the marital problems begin?"

Lisa said, "I confronted Derek for staying at his aunt's house too long after we got married. He wasn't happy about that. Shortly afterwards I told him I didn't trust him because he had become cold and distant."

Dr. Daniels explained, "You shattered his fantasy of what marriage is. You were more of a fantasy to him. He believes marriage should go one way, and when it doesn't, he wants out. You shattered him by telling him that you didn't trust him. Although, his behavior contributed to your lack of trust, correct?"

Lisa said, "Of course."

Dr. Daniels continued, "Men with PPD are cold and distant in their relationships, and they are controlling. He can't see his role in relationships or how he contributes to problems and conflicts and he probably believes he is always right."

Lisa yelped with excitement, "Yes. Dr. Daniels, Yes! If you met him, you would believe he was on the cross with Jesus. He represents this image he has created very well. He can fool the best of them."

Dr. Daniels and Lisa shared a good laugh.

Dr. Daniels affirmed what Lisa had been thinking, "You can do better, and you deserve better. Being married to a person like that is draining. He's playing the games and pulling the strings and you're the puppet."

Lisa said, "Derek would start arguments. It was like he got pleasure from arguments."

Dr. Daniels stated, "I'm not surprised. Your husband is a textbook case for PPD, but there is no cure. Derek sounds hostile, stubborn, and argumentative."

Lisa said, "Indeed, he's hostile, stubborn, and argumentative. He thrives off of confusion. I just thought he was the devil." They laughed again.

Lisa was getting her joy back one day at a time. She never argued with Derek, and he was a liar if he told anyone she did. She would have loved to record their phone calls for her own personal proof. She was overjoyed, because she didn't want to be judgmental. However, she knew Derek was unstable. There were times Derek would call her awful names but deny that he ever said anything.

Derek talked Lisa out of filing for divorce because he wanted to work things out. His insensitivity and self-centeredness shined through until the very end. Just like the narcissist he was, Derek had to end the marriage first. He controlled the narrative.

One month went past before Derek reached out to Lisa. He asked if she had received divorce papers in the mail because he had been to his attorney's office. He mailed Lisa's shoes, loofah, and his wedding band. Lisa fell over with laughter and said, "I could have bought another loofah, and I own more than three hundred pair of shoes, but thanks."

Derek didn't want the divorce when Lisa suggested it. He had to file for it first. He had to end relationships first; this empowered him. Derek began taunting Lisa. This was all fun and games to him. He didn't like her talking to the people from his church. He called and was yelling, "I can't believe you talked to people at my church! You're petty! You're pathetic! I don't give a f###!" Derek slammed the phone down in his typical manner.

Lisa shook her head and said, "Okay, God. I'm not yelling, screaming, and calling him names. I don't see a Scripture for this, but I'm going to light his butt up. I'm not going to be "too many more manipulative, fake-ass" woman of God, "not the woman you said you were" type of chick."

There were a series of ugly phone calls in between time. Derek loved the sound of crying on the other end of the phone. Lisa could hear him smiling through the phone because he spent years crying over his ex-wife and other women he lost, but he finally heard tears. Derek had finally gotten revenge on someone. Lisa wasn't comfortable talking to Derek; therefore, she emailed him.

July 28, 1:55 p.m.
From: Lisa Davis
To: Derek Davis
Subject: How Long Should I Expect Divorce Papers?

Derek,

I am so sorry you're full of hate towards me. I pray that you find a wife that God has for you. I thank you for opening my heart to the possibility of love. I was really dead to love, but I know I'm capable of loving someone other than myself. I love you and God bless.

Love,

Lisa

This marriage was stressful and weighed heavily on Lisa's mental state. She was confused because praying women were telling her to fight for her marriage, but she realized this marriage was dead. She became as psychotic as the man she married. Lisa was pathetic and felt like a failure. Another divorce. Maybe she should reconsider.

July 28, 2:41 p.m.
From: Lisa Davis
To: Derek Davis
Subject: I Don't Want a Divorce.

I'm pissed and tired of the name-calling. I'm confused. I want a divorce but don't want a divorce. You keep calling me a liar but can't tell me what I've lied about. I'm really confused at all of this name-calling. I can't stop you from divorcing me, but you can't tell me anything without calling me ugly names. You said I was just desperate to get married. We could have waited. I told you I'm loyal. Desperate, you aren't the only man in the world. I was doing fine by myself.

Lisa

Derek called the next day and asked, "Why haven't you signed the papers my attorney sent and mailed them back? My attorney sent the divorce papers certified mail."

Lisa said, "I haven't received any papers."

Derek yelled, "You are a liar! You just don't want to sign the papers."

Lisa hadn't received any papers, but Derek was so sure of himself. She began looking for the divorce papers in a pile of old mail. She even contacted her property manager and asked if they had signed for mail, which they had done in the past. Ms. Rosalyn said, "You don't have any papers or mail in the office."

Lisa discussed the details of this conversation with her friend and sister, Meka. Meka said, "Divorce papers would have come certified mail and you would have had to sign for them. I know because I sent my ex-husband divorce papers certified mail. Call the courthouse in Texas and ask. Divorce information is public, and the clerk will tell you if a divorce decree has been filed."

Lisa did an internet search and called the courthouse in Texas. The clerk said, "There isn't a divorce filed under the names of Derek and Lisa Davis."

Lisa asked, "Are you sure?"

The clerk said, "I'm positive."

Lisa said, "My estranged husband's attorney would have to file with your office, correct?"

The clerk replied, "Yes. There is no pending divorce on file. Maybe you can call your husband to see what type of game he's playing."

Lisa thanked the clerk and thought, *Who is the real liar and manipulator?*

Lisa became more and more pissed at all of the times Derek had called her a liar. He was lying and lying well. She did let more and more people know what she was going through as she was going through it. Some would say it was revengeful; she said it was therapy. Lisa was enduring verbal and emotional abuse. Too many women suffer in silence, and she had suffered enough. Derek was mentally unwell.

August 21, 10:55 p.m.
From: Lisa Davis
To: Derek Davis
Subject: NO Papers

Hi. Since you accused me of having divorce papers and refusing to sign them, I called the courthouse in Texas to see if you filed for divorce! There is no record of you filing for divorce. It should be on file at the courthouse. Let's be clear, I agreed to attend counseling with YOUR PASTOR and I wasn't calling your church to get them to tell you not to divorce me. That is your version of the upcoming story. I just wanted counseling like you told me you did with your ex-wife and ex-girlfriend. Why do I keep mentioning your ex-wife and ex-girlfriend? Because they were in the marriage with us. They are imbedded in my brain. I know more about them than I do you. I wanted to try before giving up completely. Per Derek, "I always fight for my relationships." Lie, you gave up within two weeks on this one. This thing with you has torn me up. Again, you lied about sending me papers that I won't sign. There aren't any papers. Go be free, little birdie. Go get remarried over and over again with your unstable behind. Nope, I'm not perfect, but I'm working on staying in right standing with God, even when no one is looking. You're a spiritual rapist on a demonic assignment from the pits of hell.

Lisa

This man had been calling Lisa out of her name for six months. Yet, she knew Derek was lying before they were married. She rationalized and justified that there was something wrong with everyone, and laughed at how foolish she had been for marrying an unstable man.

Her email confronting Derek about the "fake divorce papers" pissed him off. He rushed and filed for divorce. He had to cover his lies. Everything Derek did was calculated. He had to paint a good story for his friends. Lisa felt sorry for herself and Derek's friends because he was dishonest with himself and all of the people who supported him.

CHAPTER FIFTEEN

THE ATTORNEY'S OFFICE

Derek wasn't going to let Lisa get away with confronting him over his lie. He would make her pay. Derek would make Lisa pay. Lisa was getting into the groove of life. She had started rebuilding her relationship with God. Derek and this marriage had become her god. She was reconnecting with her one true love.

Lisa loved blasting inspirational music from her iPhone 5 while getting dressed for work. She was running late and dashed out of the door. Around lunchtime, she realized that she didn't have her cell phone. She drove home and found it in the clothes hamper and noticed she had a missed call. Lisa's gut stirred. *What's going on? This can't be good.* Lisa listened to the voicemail, which stated, "*Ms. Davis, this is Constable Johnson. I came by your house, but no one was home. I need to give you some papers.*"

Lisa hit the call-back button and identified herself as Ms. Davis. Constable Johnson said, "I have these divorce papers that I need to give you."

Lisa said, "I'm headed back to work, but I get off at 4:30 p.m. I can meet you in the parking lot of Walmart at 4:45 p.m."

Constable Johnson said, "I don't know if I'll make it back to that side of town by 4:45 p.m."

Lisa said, "We can meet tomorrow at lunch around 12 p.m."

Constable Johnson said, "I talked to your apartment manager and they said you work. Also, they said the man who sent these divorce papers must be an idiot because she's one of the kindest and most generous residents. They think highly of you and I kind of feel bad delivering the papers."

Lisa said, "It's okay. He is an idiot. We can meet tomorrow." Constable Johnson agreed.

Lisa headed to Walmart and was there at 12:00 sharp. She called Constable Johnson and told him she would be in a silver Toyota Camry with the license plates HAV 123.

Constable Johnson said, "I'm sending the papers back and they will just have to resend them. If he wants the divorce, he'll have to pay the money."

Lisa said, "Okay, but he needs to be aware that I was ready to receive the papers because he already accused me of having them."

Constable Johnson replied, "That's his problem. Good luck."

Lisa probably shouldn't have reached out to Derek, but she was tired.

September 8, 6:31 p.m.
From: Lisa Davis
To: Derek Davis

Hi,

The constable is sending the papers back. I was at work when he called, and we couldn't find the time to meet. He explained that the divorce papers will be sent back and can be rerouted through alternate means. BTW: Send them certified mail so I can read them. Since you are representing yourself, it would be interesting to see what you have put in there. You lie so much. BTW: You didn't file for divorce until after I confronted you about lying. You don't have an attorney either. You are evil. You call me dramatic, but the theatrics with the constable is a bit much. Send them certified mail so I can see what information you put in there and then I'll sign them, or better yet, I can send them in person, since I have a job in that area.

Respectfully,

Lisa

Lisa knew by suggesting Derek send the divorce papers certified mail he would resend them via constable. He loathed being told what to do and Lisa was pushing his buttons. She also knew Derek was trying to get the divorce filed before she moved to Arlington, TX. Her older and wiser counsel said that was a coward's move. "He didn't marry you through the mail, so the divorce shouldn't be completed via mail." Lisa listened, but she was over all of the madness.

One more week went by and another voicemail was left on Lisa's work phone. This time it was from the legal department where Lisa worked. The message stated, "*Hi, Ms. Davis. I'm Mr. Jackson at legal. Someone called to see how a constable can get divorce papers to you. Call me back at 555- 6788.*" Lisa returned Mr. Jackson's call. She said, "I just heard your message and wanted to see what I needed to do."

Mr. Jackson, "This individual wants a divorce really badly. At any rate, you work in a secure location and we wouldn't allow the constable to deliver papers to you."

Lisa asked, "What do you suggest? Because it's time to get this mess over with."

Mr. Jackson said, "We can call the office back and you can meet the constable at the legal office at 1:00 p.m."

Lisa said, "I'll let my supervisor know I'll need to be at the legal office tomorrow at 1:00 pm." She informed Dr. Sterling, who was also a psychologist, that she had to meet the constable at legal tomorrow at 1:00 p.m.

Dr. Sterling said, "He really wants out of the marriage, huh? He didn't give it a chance. He sounds like someone with a personality disorder."

Lisa said, "You're correct, but that's just the tip of the iceberg."

Dr. Sterling said, "He's really trying to hurt and humiliate you."

Lisa said, "It's his way of getting back at me for telling mutual people about our problems, especially his pastor. I endured verbal and emotional abuse the entire length of this joke of a marriage. I don't care if anyone believes me or not. A woman always has to defend her truth against a man's lie. Plus, perception is everything to him. He has to win. In his mind, he filed for divorce first, so he won. He'll be able to tell his friends, family, church members, and coworkers that he left that crazy-ass lady. His support system is as dumb as I am because they are too dumb to see how disturbed he is."

Dr. Sterling said, "I'm definitely hearing Axis II, and it's best that he becomes another woman's problem. You don't need that type of stress. Some women are built for that level of drama. That isn't your character or personality. Good riddance."

Lisa said, "I don't think another woman should have to endure this level of foolery. Just plain old tomfoolery. I feel sorry for the next victim. Well, we need to reschedule our clients, so I can meet with the constable. I'm ready to begin my healing process."

Lisa discussed the recent events with Linda and Stacy. All three of them were having marital problems. Lisa had been married for twenty years, and Stacy had been married for fifteen years.

Linda said, "You kept saying Derek had an evil presence, but I laughed every time because I didn't believe it. You kept saying that man was broken but he was projecting unto you."

Stacy said, "I hope he heals from the inside before he destroys another woman."

Lisa, Linda, and Stacy were silent. None wanted to put too much thought into what was going on. They didn't want to say the wrong things. When all else failed, they prayed. They prayed for the healing of hearts, marriages, forgiveness, and restoration of marriages.

Lisa slept peacefully. She woke up and dressed nicely, and was ready to get this portion of her life over with. She worked diligently while watching the clock. Come on, 1:00 p.m; come on. Let's get these papers signed. She dashed out of the door at 12:30 p.m. because she wasn't going to miss the constable. *Let's give Nabal that divorce.*

Lisa arrived, and Attorney Smith said, "I didn't recognize your name. Are you waiting on the constable?"

Lisa replied, "Yes ma'am."

Attorney Smith said, "I don't think I want to get married. Too many people I know are getting a divorce."

Lisa said, "The institution of marriage isn't bad. It's the philosophy of the person you marry that makes it bad."

Attorney Smith asked, "Are you ready to move forward?"

Lisa said, "Yes. It's not much to move forward from. We didn't get to know each other. The transition will get better. Are you going to be here when the constable arrives? Because the estranged husband has already lied like I was holding on to the papers and refusing to sign them."

Attorney Smith said, "I'll be right here." She walked Lisa across the hall so that she could sit comfortably and wait because she had business to conduct.

Lisa watched her cell phone. It was 12:50, 51, 52, 53, 54, 55, 56, 57, 58, and 59. Lisa was anxious, "Come on, Constable, let's get this show on the road." It was now 1:00 p.m. The constable hadn't shown. It was 1:15 p.m., and no constable. One thirty p.m.; still no constable. The attorney called the front gate to see if the constable was stuck in traffic because he should have been there by now. Security didn't recall seeing a constable come through the gate, nor did he see a car at the entrance. The attorney and security guard began making calls to see if anyone had seen a constable. It was now 2:00 p.m.

Attorney Smith said, "I'm leaving at 3 p.m. today. If you want to wait, you can, but he should have been here by now because our office coordinated this on yesterday with an ETA of 1:00 p.m."

Lisa texted her supervisor and told her the constable hadn't arrived, but she was going to wait. Her supervisor told her to hang out for the rest of the afternoon if she wanted to, because she was going home. It was now 3:00 p.m. and no constable. Attorney Smith asked Lisa to leave her phone number with the clerk just in case he showed up. Lisa provided the clerk with her info and told him that if the constable arrived, call and she would be there in five minutes.

Lisa went back to her office and continued watching the clock. The clerk called and said, "We closed our building at 4 p.m., and no one has come." Lisa thanked the clerk and told him to have a good weekend. Lisa thought that was odd. Derek had sent divorce papers twice by a constable and neither attempt was successful.

Lisa laughed. She shared this information with Evangelists Clark and Thomas. Evangelist Clark believed, "God is blocking the divorce." Lisa didn't agree with her and remained quiet.

Evangelist Thomas said, "No, what God has done is protected her from being embarrassed. Her husband's heart is stone and full of evil. He has humiliated her during the marriage and wanted to do the grand finale, but God blocked it. His motives were evil from the beginning."

Evangelist Thomas began speaking in her heavenly language. All three of them began worshipping God. Evangelist Thomas said, "Lisa, you had to go through this. God has shown me that your husband has a call on his life, but he's running from God. He has begged for the right wife and told God he would be obedient if he had the right wife. You were the right wife, but he didn't want you; nor was he ready to live completely for Christ. He likes being in the bed with women, going to church, and giving the appearance of being a man of God. You had to go through this. Another woman may have committed suicide after being verbally, mentally, and emotionally abused. God knew you would hurt, but He knew you would heal."

Lisa was on the phone, and her eyes were bigger than saucers because she had never met Evangelist Thomas. Evangelist Thomas continued, "You have a women's ministry and a marriage ministry in you. Sometimes God has to let us go to hell and back in order to do what He has called us to do. That man has so much pride, and he would have continued wearing you down. I have a friend who is a minister, and he has been married four times. He keeps blaming the women. I finally told him that he was the problem, that he was the broken one, and he kept hurting women. There are plenty of broken men out there, and you married one. Don't worry. God will clean him up after this. He hurt you on purpose, and God will deal with him accordingly."

Lisa thanked Evangelists Clark and Thomas for their continued support, no judgment or condemnation.

Evangelist Clark said, "You should have been keeping a diary of every name he called you, every time he slammed the phone down, and every disgusting thing he did so that you can write a book. See, it's women out there who are waiting on a godly man and are being deceived and broken. Women need to hear how Derek gave off the appearance of God, but behind closed doors, he was a monster. There are a lot of women suffering in silence."

Evangelist Thomas interjected, "Do you know what my ministry is?"

"No ma'am, I don't," was Lisa's reply.

Evangelist Thomas said, "I help women who have been physically and mentally abused. These men are hurting daughters of Zion, and they need help getting free and delivered from the residue of this type of violence. Rest, because God knows his address. This man wasn't ready to get married. Of course, he will blame you, but he wasn't ready to get married. Better yet, he wants to be married, but not to you. He will never apologize to you because I detect a stubborn and prideful streak. I can almost see him smiling for the damage he feels he has done. He won't be smiling when God shows up at his house."

Lisa said, "I knew I wasn't completely crazy. Derek was attentive premarriage and became so cold after the marriage."

Evangelist Thomas said, "He's an abuser. He was going to destroy your self-esteem one day at a time."

Lisa was so happy to have wise women in her circle. Lord knows, everyone needs support when going through trauma. Lisa thought about what Evangelist Thomas had said about God blocking Derek's attempt to embarrass her at work. God is awesome. She also recognized that she was the victim of verbal and emotional abuse and began researching everything about emotional abuse. She had studied psychology in college and was familiar with domestic abuse. She wasn't an expert at either.

Lisa knew from the onset that Derek was a bit challenged, but she ignored the red, blue, and orange flags. In hindsight, when Derek and Lisa were discussing her big move from Oklahoma City to Arlington, TX, she would often tell him how she loved to go places, especially on the weekend. Derek would say things like, "No, you aren't. I don't move my car when I don't have to. That's wasting gas."

Lisa said, "No, I'm going to continue doing the things I like to do."

Derek said, "No, you'll be with me doing things I like to do."

Lisa ignored everything. It was right in her face. The only thing they had in common was sex.

Lisa's internet research revealed what she already knew. She was one of the many faces of domestic abuse. Derek made Lisa feel guilty about everything. He was judgmental and never acknowledged her hurt. According to healthyplace.com, "Emotional abuse is defined as any act, including confinement, isolation, verbal assault, intimidation, infantilization, or any other treatment, which may diminish the sense of identity, dignity, and self-worth. Signs of emotional abuse include: yelling, name-calling, ignoring, humiliation, denial of the abuse, and blaming the victim. One partner does this in order to show dominance. The abuser then begins to fantasize about abusing his partner again and sets up a situation in which more emotional abuse can take place."

Lisa thought to herself, *Oh no! How could this be?* She had endured months of verbal abuse and began reflecting on other incidents. Although Lisa made more money than Derek, he wanted her in his environment. Derek's company could have transferred him to a department in Oklahoma City. He became angry and informed Lisa that he didn't like Oklahoma and that she was supposed to move where he was. He wasn't willing to compromise. It was going to be Derek's way or no way.

Lisa married the same man twenty years apart—different names, but similar personalities. She had to gut out that thing that had attracted this level of stupidity twice. Her mind was racing, but she continued reading about emotional abuse.

"Emotional abusers make you doubt yourself. Sometimes an emotional abuser will lie to you in order to confuse you, in order to make you doubt yourself, your perceptions, or memory. Sometimes they will attack your ability to see right from wrong. Emotional abusers give and take away. For example: if you are with a spouse who loves you, you feel all is right in the world, and you feel like your spouse has your back. By contrast, if you are in a marriage/relationship with an emotional abuser, you are consistently thinking of ways not to offend, insult, irritate, or make your partner angry."

Lisa used to walk on eggshells. She tried not to offend or insult Derek in order to keep the peace. She was indeed a victim.

Lisa wept for the millions of women who were suffering in silence. She wept for the millions of women without a voice. She wept for herself and for her freedom. Lisa's cousin called with another sermon on how a praying wife can change her husband. Lisa didn't want to hear anything else about her role as a wife. She was more concerned about her mind, spirit, and soul. Many people were encouraging her to fight for her marriage, but God was showing her something different. She was no longer going to pray for a man who didn't want to be with her.

Lisa would pray for Derek's deliverance, but not restoration. God was clear whereas people were clouding her thought process. The job offer Lisa received in Arlington, TX, was rejected. She had found an apartment in Arlington, TX, and hired movers. She was going to take the federal job, work one year, and move to South or North Carolina. Needless to say, God blocked the move. Lisa had typed her two-weeks' notice and was set to turn it in the following Monday. She was getting dressed when she saw her phone light up.

Lisa answered. It was the hiring manager. He said, "Good morning Ms. Davis. I have some bad news. Tell me you haven't turned in your notice, because I would hate for you not to have a job."

Lisa said, "I was going to turn it in this morning."

Mr. Goodman said, "I screwed up and my boss caught it Friday evening. I am so sorry."

Lisa said, "No, don't be sorry. God has a plan. I still have a job, so it worked out."

Mr. Goodman said, "Your résumé says you live in Oklahoma. Why did you want to move to Arlington?"

Lisa said, "My soon-to-be ex-husband is there. Initially, I was moving to be with him, reconcile or whatever, but God has blocked it all."

Mr. Goodman asked, "How long were you married?"

Lisa said, "Technically, two weeks. We got along pretty well, but it went downhill after that. Maybe three months of confusion and another two months of drama."

Mr. Goodman said, "Well, it was better that is was only three months rather than three years or thirty years. See, y'all women got to start marrying men of faith."

Lisa laughed, "Mr. Goodman, not only is he this so-called man of faith, but he's in a leadership position in his church."

Mr. Goodman said, "Well, that happens because some churches don't hold their leaders accountable. I know of churches where the ministers are sleeping with the prophetesses, the ushers, and deaconesses. God may be sparing you from connecting to a church where there is no growth. God is very protective of HIS children and HE won't let you go too far out of HIS will. Can I tell my wife about you? Because I feel like you are special and have an anointing on your life that the enemy is trying to destroy. My wife and I have been married twenty-eight years, and we believe in marriage, but with the right spouse."

Lisa said, "Thanks, and tell her I will accept all prayers."

Lisa tore up her notice and sighed a sigh of relief. She sat at her desk and gave thanks to God for protection and provision. Linda knocked and entered Lisa's office.

Linda asked, "How are things? Are you excited about turning in your notice? I'm so happy you'll be getting away from the Wicked Witch of the West."

Lisa said, "Well, God blocked the divorce papers on Friday, and He also blocked the move." Linda looked confused.

Lisa continued, "Mr. Goodman called this morning and said he made a mistake by giving me the position. His boss caught it on Friday evening, and he wanted to catch me before I became jobless."

Linda was vexed, "Report him, because that was a stupid mistake."

Lisa said, "No, that was God blocking me from enemy territory. I would have been moving near him and his supporters. I would have been in a church where there was no growth. His church is performance based. God saw what I would possibly have to endure, and God knows I'm not against shooting a person if I had to." Linda and Lisa laughed.

Linda said, "I'm amazed at your strength. You cry, laugh, and keep moving. You kept saying this man didn't want you. You said it two weeks after you were married. I feel bad because I kept telling you that y'all had to grow together. You kept saying something wasn't right, and that something shifted after the marriage. Dang it. I feel bad for encouraging you to fight for your marriage. You knew something wasn't right and all of us kept telling you to stop overthinking."

Lisa said, "Yes, I knew something wasn't right. When I looked into his eyes, they were distant and cold."

Linda said, "At least you are going to be free. I'm still in mine."

Lisa said, "Make a choice. God forgives, even for divorce."

Linda exited the office. Lisa said out loud and proud, "I'm free! The stress of having a husband is no more. Now I can heal." She carried on her daily routine. Most of her clients noticed she wasn't wearing her wedding ring. Lisa smiled.

She had already pawned her and Derek's rings. She got a nice amount of money for Derek's ring, as well she should. She paid $5,000 for his ring, which was way more than Derek spent on her ring. Lisa reflected that she had been in that relationship by herself from beginning to end. She laughed inwardly. She sang the lyrics to an oldie but goodie, *It takes a fool to learn that love don't love nobody.* Love isn't the problem. It's the people you choose to do your love walk with.

There was a song for every occasion. In honor of this occasion, Lisa celebrated to a song her friend told her about in 2005, "New Day," by Patti Labelle. She belted out the lyrics as if she were trying out for "The Voice." She sang, "Seems my life is finally coming together. Feels so good, don't think I've ever been better. It's clear to me my future will bring the peace I've been longing for is mine forever more. It's a new day." Yes, Ms. Patti. Lisa was spreading her wings. She was getting back to her happy place.

After Lisa's session with a client, Mr. Anthony entered the office. Mr. Anthony, who wasn't shy, said, "I heard you were going through a divorce. That was quick."

Lisa smiled, "It is well."

Mr. Anthony asked, "Is it too much to ask what happened in such a short time?"

Lisa gave him an abbreviated version of what had taken place.

Mr. Anthony said, "That doesn't make sense. I'm a man, and that joker was playing games. He started off texting and calling, but stopped after you married him. That's game, baby. Typical of an insecure man. He was breaking you down, Tina."

Lisa asked, "Who is Tina?"

Mr. Anthony said, "You, Tina Turner. Ike was breaking you down emotionally and next comes the physical abuse. Every time you called he was probably like, 'Yeah, I got this woman in my pocket. I'm not calling her or responding. Let her chase me.' I'm a man and I recognize game." Lisa laughed.

Mr. Anthony asked, "What do his friends say?"

Lisa said, "He doesn't have many friends. He has two female friends from high school and one he met along the way. Plus, one male friend. He talks to a lot of women at his church."

Mr. Anthony said, "Humph. One male friend, huh? Classic." Lisa looked but didn't respond. Mr. Anthony continued, "He's a classic player. He keeps women in his life in order to learn what a woman likes/dislikes. Women are nurturers. Women probably feel sorry for him, and tell him he will meet the right woman. They probably tell him what they don't like about their men and he listens. He probably gives good advice based off of the conversations he has had with other women. He's a master manipulator. He changes with every woman he meets. I can guarantee his male friend is probably whorish and sleeps with multiple women. He looks like a good man in comparison. Women love his company. It's game, baby. The game wasn't fun with you. He needs complete control. Somewhere along the way, you saw something he didn't want you to see and that lessened his attraction to you. All he will do now is tell his female friends how crazy you are, they will coddle him, and he will do a better job of fooling the next woman. He's insecure."

Lisa said, "No, according to him, that would be me."

Mr. Anthony said, "No, that was game too. Real men will love a woman through her insecurities, but boys love to chip away at a woman's self-esteem. He's insecure. Only insecure men hang around a bunch of women because male friends would call him out on his bull####. I don't understand y'all women. What woman would be his friend when he's clearly dogging other women out?"

Lisa said, "They have only heard his version of every relationship."

Mr. Anthony said, "Again, most women don't have the insight to ask what he's doing or not doing. Don't ever date a man who only has female friends ever again. Meet his friends next time in advance. See how their relationships are before you marry again. Most people hang around people who they are most alike. If all of his friends are in raggedy relationships, the blind is leading the blind. Think about it."

Lisa smiled, but those words resonated. She sat thinking about the dynamics of Derek's friends and their relationships. She felt sorry for his friends. He badmouthed them as much as he had badmouthed everyone else in his life. He wasn't faithful to his friends.

CHAPTER SIXTEEN

WHY SHOULD I BE EMBARRASSED?

A lot of women won't know they are married to a narcissist until it's too late. Lisa went home, drank a bottle of wine, and exhaled. She made a mistake. She ignored the warning signs. She took God's quietness for a yes. Lisa realized that with the recent turn of events, God allowed her to fall, not fail. There is no failure in God. Different people kept telling her to pray for her husband because "God is going to charge you if you don't." She would continue to pray, but divorce was imminent.

Lisa looked up to heaven and prayed, "God, I'll take a beating for this one, but I don't want Derek back, not even if he's delivered. I pray Derek is healed before he wounds another woman. I pray he repents for the seeds he's planting. I pray Derek learns the role of a husband and a wife. I pray a prophet will cross his path and speak into his spirit. That job is too much for mere humans. A woman can't be responsible for his happiness. I pray that You'll send godly men to help teach him how to be a man. God, I repent. I thought I was making a godly decision, but You know what's best."

Lisa was raw and honest before God. She cried and screamed, but she didn't recognize that scream. It was one of pain, repentance, and redemption. "God, I'm so confused. I've been confused since I married Derek. God, You know Derek was meaner than a rattlesnake. I never raised my voice at him. I called him names behind his back but kept it free from name-calling in an effort to be a good wife. God, I was tired. I was tired of the verbal abuse. I was tired of the stress. I was tired of the rejection and neglect. I was tired of feeling unloved and unwanted. He wasn't the one for me. He should have been a friend, not a husband. He was supposed to be an assignment, but I married him. I have failed You, God, but thank YOU for blocking the divorce papers from coming to my job and thank YOU for stopping me from going to Texas.

"You are an amazing God. I love YOU, Lord, and I had stopped serving YOU while I was caught up in that foolery. Being with Derek distracted me from YOU. He became my god. I was no longer connected to YOU. He wasn't worthy of taking YOUR place. HE couldn't love me, provide for me, protect me, or carry me like YOU. How could I allow a mere man to replace the one true, living God? I'm so sorry, Lord. Thank YOU for allowing this hurt to happen. Thank YOU for allowing this humiliation to happen. Many are the afflictions of the righteous, but YOU deliver us out of them all. YOU have delivered me out of this, and I thank YOU. Amen and Amen."

Lisa heard a voice, "Get up. Wipe your face. He's gone." Lisa dried her eyes, got up, and didn't shed another tear. She was so excited. Lisa felt a kinship to King David. David mourned before his son died. After the death of his son, David carried on, and so did Lisa. Lisa had a good weekend. She unpacked her boxes and resettled into her apartment with a huge smile on her face. She planned to call the courthouse first thing Monday morning to see what she needed to do.

Evangelist Clark called on Saturday morning and said, "You sound happy."

Lisa responded, "I am happy."

"What's going on with the divorce? Evangelist Clark asked.

Lisa said, "I'll be calling the courthouse on Monday for further instructions."

"God may have blocked it," said Evangelist Clark with hope.

Lisa was tired of the "God blocked it" talk. She wasn't tired of God, but tired of people thinking they knew what God was thinking. This marriage was over before it started. After all, God had told her to get up. Lisa decided to listen to God, not people. She said, "Divorce isn't the end of the world. If Derek is the only man God has for me, I'll pass."

Evangelist Clark began quoting Scriptures, but Lisa tuned her out. She knew what the Word said. She also knew God doesn't mess with free will. Regardless of what others hoped to see, this marriage had met its fate. Lisa laughed inwardly. She loved Evangelist Clark, but she wasn't feeling her this morning.

Evangelist Clark said, "God can clean him up and make him apologize."

Lisa said, "Evangelist Clark, I'm fine. My life is getting back to where it should have stayed…with God."

Monday morning couldn't arrive fast enough. Lisa was ready to call the courthouse. She headed to the office and called the courthouse at 8:00 a.m. sharp. She identified herself to the clerk and asked what she needed to do in order to complete the divorce.

The clerk said, "The court date is set for the second of October."

Lisa said, "Court? Do I have to show up? I really don't want to look the enemy in his face. I might smack his assets and end up in jail." The clerk laughed.

Lisa said, "No, seriously. I would rather go out on a high note. Wait, can you tell me what's in the divorce decree?"

The clerk said, "You can request a copy and it's ten cents per page."

Lisa said, "I'm not sending a dime. I've wasted enough resources on this marriage. Can you tell me if he put anything mean or what he filed under?"

The clerk searched her file. She revealed, "Irreconcilable differences, but nothing else."

Lisa asked, "He isn't asking for spousal support or any financial payment for emotional suffering, is he?"

The clerk laughed and replied, "No, it's cut and dry."

Lisa said, "Since I'm in Oklahoma and don't want to spend my hard-earned money on entertaining Nabal, what do I need to do?"

The clerk advised her to type a note to the judge and tell him that she agreed to the terms of the divorce and wasn't going to contest it.

"Awesome!" Lisa exclaimed.

The clerk said, "Fax it to 682-555-9546 and put ATTN: Clerk's Office."

Lisa immediately typed a note that said,

To Whom It May Concern:

I am equally as ready to end this divorce and won't contest it. Goodbye and good riddance, Mr. Davis.

God Bless,

Lisa Dixon

Just like that, the divorce was granted. Lisa never requested a copy of the divorce decree; she couldn't care less. She was free. Derek had abandoned her. She was completely free. Lisa received so much support from people of faith. The well-wishes and encouragement were a blessing. She knew she would be all right. Lisa also heard about the naysayers and gossipers. She laughed.

Debra said, "I don't put stuff on Facebook and fool with too many people. You know how these folks in Little Rock are. All they do is talk about you. I feel so bad for you because you posted pictures of you and him, and he never posted any pictures of you and him. He never changed his Facebook status to married. He never acknowledged you unless it was negative."

Lisa said, "Let me give the people of Little Rock something to talk about."

Good Afternoon, Facebookers,

This year has been challenging, humiliating, and a lesson. I got married and divorced all in the same year. Some of my friends said they felt sorry for me because I put all of my business on Facebook by posting our wedding pictures and changing my status to married, but he never posted any pictures nor changed his status. There is no reason for me to be embarrassed. I entered this marriage for the right reasons and got dumped. Why should I be embarrassed? My motives were pure. Don't feel sorry for me. Pray for him. Be Blessed, Bookers.

Lisa wasn't ashamed of her experiences, whether good or bad. She willingly shared them. The folks on Facebook, family, or friends didn't have a heaven or hell to put her in. She just added a little more fuel to the fire. Surprisingly, people didn't pry. They offered encouragement and life went on.

Lisa blocked all people connected to Derek. He had already accused her of stalking his ex-girlfriend's page, whose name she didn't know; therefore, Lisa didn't want to feed his paranoia by staying in touch with anyone he was close to. He would swear Lisa was trying to keep an eye on him or get back with him. She didn't want to see anyone tagging his name in pictures or posts. She didn't want to know if he was alive or dead.

Some people said, "That's so petty and childish." That was their opinion. They had never been with a narcissist. Lisa didn't try to stay connected to anyone she slept with. They didn't have any ties to each other, so what was the purpose? She was positive that her and Derek's mutual friends thought she was angry with them because she disconnected from them as well. They were wrong too. Lisa didn't want to destroy any more relationships.

Derek had spoken badly about a lot of people. If they defended him, Lisa would have had to tell them an ugly truth. She would rather they kept their friendships with Derek. She was going to be fine, and they could think whatever they wanted.

Early on, Lisa did struggle with whether or not Derek's friends would believe his lies. On the flip side, she recognized that even Charles Manson had supporters. Enough said. Derek would always have his cheerleaders, but so would Lisa. Everyone has cheerleaders and critics. Lisa had opened herself up to both.

One of Lisa's cousins said, "That boy's eyes were shady. When I saw his picture, I knew it wouldn't work. He's a sneaky character."

Another friend, "I can't believe you let him fool you. You have been too faithful to God and you let that boy fool you. It wouldn't be me. I would have seen right through him. Can't no man fool me."

Monica said, "Derek didn't know you loved him. We have never heard you cry over a man."

Lisa realized Derek didn't love himself. She wondered if the tears were more for herself or him. Regardless, the chapter was closing and there was no point trying to rationalize about the marriage. Lisa had to be honest with God and herself. She didn't want to move to the area where Derek lived. She most definitely didn't want to live in that antiquated home of his.

Lisa opened up at church and to other people. The more she shared her experiences, the more she realized she wasn't alone. One lady shared she was a virgin until she was married. She dated the guy for one year. They went to church together, prayed, and did everything God told them to do. They had a big wedding and an exotic honeymoon in Cancún. Shortly after returning home, he left. She never heard from him again.

Lisa began hearing more and more stories of pastors, elders, deacons, men of God who were wooing women, marrying them, and leaving after having sex with them. All of them were spiritual rapists, in Lisa's opinion. They were raping God's daughters without a conscience. Have mercy on their souls, Lord.

Lisa began posting on marriage, divorce, and walking out the healing process. She was invited to speak at a women's conference at Mission Deliverance Christian Center. She didn't want to speak because she felt she failed. She'd recently spoken at a conference about the significance of waiting on a godly husband, and exactly eight months later, she was about to share the pain of divorce. Lisa reluctantly agreed.

First Lady Binder said, "I really believe the women need to hear about your experiences. Don't let the devil keep you ashamed and in bondage. We go through things for other people."

Lisa agreed to speak at the conference. She fasted and prayed and asked the Lord what He would have her to speak about. She didn't want to bash Derek, but she also wanted women to know that marrying a "godly" man doesn't divorce-proof a marriage. There are plenty of undelivered "godly" men from the pulpit to the pew. As Lisa was studying, she heard, "There is a snake in my garden."

That's it! That's it! Thank YOU, Holy Spirit! That is a great subject. Scripture reading would come from Genesis 3:1-24. Lisa was excited. The devil meant it for bad, but God turned it into something good. Won't HE do it? Yes, HE will.

Notes from Lisa's sermon:

You betta (not better) but betta pray about it, because there can be a snake in your garden. Satan appeared in the Garden of Eden in the form of a serpent. You see, Satan isn't a serpent, but he disguised himself as one. Satan will always come in the form of something we desire, but we don't feel the sting of his venom until it's too late. In this season, let us be careful who we allow in our garden!

I know from experience, because the man I married presented himself as a "godly" man, but he turned out to be the husband from hell. He may say the same thing about me, but God will silence HIS lies. He was selfish, self-centered, self-righteous, and full of pride. Premarriage he was loving, kind, and even tempered. We prayed, fasted, and read the Word together premarriage. We got married, and I said something he didn't like. The marriage was over, but I didn't know it at the time.

Unbeknownst to me, he had already told his family he wasn't happy with me. I was on cloud nine. He started to withdraw from me, and he no longer wanted to read the Word or pray with me. His response was, "I don't need to read the Word with you. I can study on my own."

I saw a woman in a dream that he was attached to. I began praying against that spirit. The harder I prayed, the more he bragged about his ex-wife and how much money she was making and the kind of car she drove. I don't know about you, but it's tacky to brag about an ex to your current spouse. However, he called me insecure. No. He was disrespectful.

My friends laughed when I told them that a demon had attached itself to Derek. It had to be a demon. I didn't want to believe that I married a mentally disturbed person on purpose. Unfortunately, I had married a mentally unstable man. I endured emotional abuse with this man. No unsaved man has ever talked to me the way Derek did. This is the first "believer" I had dated, but will be careful about the next one.

Emotional abuse in a marriage is a covert form of domestic violence and type of abuse, and many women aren't able to recognize that they are a victim. One month after being married, I was sad, nervous, and sick, and became fearful to talk to my husband. He used emotional abuse to control, manipulate, and degrade me. He called me names, but he was projecting who he was unto me. He wouldn't talk to me for days. He held grudges and would never apologize for anything.

He always felt good about how he treated me. He had this self-satisfying grin that would have made a violent woman smack him right across his face. Derek said he wasn't happy with me and didn't enjoy being married to me. I flipped the script and

asked, "What must I do to make sure you are happy with me?"
He didn't answer. He couldn't answer. It was a deafening silence
on the other end of the line. He was looking for a way out. He
really didn't have anything. I wasn't perfect, but I certainly wasn't
as damaged as Derek tried to make me out to be.

He played so many mind games. He would say he called but I
didn't answer the phone. I didn't see any missed calls, but he swore
I was the liar. I really began to think I was crazy. Derek could sell
a bike to a man with one leg. He had a great external character.
Heck, no one who knew him would even believe he was mean.

Now I understand why women who are physically abused
remain silent. The perpetrator is usually churchgoing, mild
mannered, pleasant, and charming, with stellar character. They
can fool a person with three eyes. Just in case some of you are
dating and thinking about marriage, and to those of you who are
married, here are some tactics used by an emotional abuser:

A.) Isolation from friends and family (Derek began telling
me I was talking to my friends too much and was putting them
before him).

B.) Discourages independent activities that don't involve them
(Derek said he wanted me to spend all of my time with him, he
wanted me to go to the mall with him, and everything was about
him).

C.) Constantly criticizes, belittles, or demeans (Derek never
complimented me. He bragged on his exes and talked about how
fine and pretty they were).

D.) They hold grudges and don't forgive. They are stubborn
and intimidating.

E.) They will try to make all of the decisions. Derek was
choking the life out of me. Anything I said was met with dismissal.
My feelings didn't matter.

I can laugh now, but I believe Derek's interpretation of the Scripture was, "She who finds Derek finds a good thing and obtains favor from the Lord."

"The enemy comes to steal, kill, and to destroy" (John 10:10). He comes to steal your joy, peace, and happiness; kill your character; and destroy your destiny. He will come in the form of a husband, but God.

I realized that some men don't do much within the marriage because all of the books are geared towards being A Good Wife, How to Love Your Husband, Build Your Husband, Love Your Husband, How to Be a Proverbs 31 Woman, and so forth. I believe men have some responsibility in the marriage. With authority comes responsibility.

I didn't want to get divorced after three months. I fasted, prayed, and begged my husband. That didn't matter. There was nothing I could have done. You can't make a man stay with you, and neither will God. It has to be his decision.

As a matter of fact, the more I prayed, the more manipulative he became. He would call me, yelling and screaming, and slam down the phone. He wouldn't answer the phone when I called. He did this often, and it was draining. The cycle went from waiting, hoping, hurting, anger, forgiveness, forgetting, and again.

This man called me a whore, like his ex-wife and ex-girlfriend. I had been holding my tongue, not arguing or yelling. This made me angry. I still didn't argue. I drafted an email that said,

"Who have you caught me in bed with? I was celibate before you. You are the one who has been sleeping with women in your church. You know that you are a coward. You were right; I was desperate because per your conversation you chased the other women but I'm chasing you. I loved you without conditions but I'm the whore and the liar. Since I'm like your ex-wife, which bill did you pay?

Which master's degree did you pay for? What house did you put me in? I was maintaining financially and educationally before I met you and will continue to do so. You said you felt trapped in this marriage.

How and why did I trap you? I make more money than you. You said, the Holy Spirit told you I didn't love you. Honey, it was a spirit, but it wasn't holy. I really thought God had blessed me with a man of God who could protect me, but instead I got a confused little boy who was still licking his wounds from his momma, ex-wife, and ex-girlfriends. You need to forgive your ex-wife and reconcile with her because you are destroying women."

Ladies, the devil is loose and looking for you. You betta be careful because there could be a snake in your garden. Ladies, I felt like I was spiritually raped. I felt like Tamar after being raped by her brother, Amnon (2 Samuel 13:1-22). I felt dirty, unclean, ashamed, and guilty after marrying Derek. He gets the empathy; I get the blame. I'm learning to trust God even when I can't trace HIM. My betrayal wasn't to make me bitter but to make me better.

Ladies, don't make the same mistake I made. Don't think because a man is "into" church that he's "into" God. I reached out to his pastor and first lady for help. They didn't respond. They are equally as guilty for allowing that type of foolishness to take place under their leadership. Derek always said my pastor didn't judge us. I was really disturbed by that statement.

Derek's pastor isn't holding his leaders accountable for their behavior. I told Derek I need accountability and correction. I don't want anyone to experience this level of hurt and confusion. I believed his friends who said he was a good man. His friends haven't slept with him, so what do they know?

I'll never take someone else's word for someone else's character after this experience. The most important lesson I gathered from this marriage is that learning is a gift, even if pain is the teacher.

The room was quiet; facial expressions ranged from sadness, empathy, compassion, understanding, anger, and reflection. The applause came shortly afterwards. Many women shared their experiences with men in the church.

Most of them had been married to pastors, deacons, and ministers who were verbally and physically abusive and master manipulators. Their husbands used the Word of God to keep the women in line or make them feel guilty. Lisa's story wasn't isolated. There are many. There are many women who were silent because it was an embarrassment to the church if you spoke up.

Lisa didn't get that memo. These men needed help. They needed deliverance, but no one was willing to help them. Lisa supposed people had to be willing to admit they had a problem before they could receive help. Apostle Byrd said, "Let us pray over this woman of God before service concludes. Woman of God, I heard your pain. You poured out and you'll be fine. One thing I heard you say, you worked on being a wife. You read books; you studied the Word. You weren't specific in the type of husband you wanted.

I feel he loves you, but he wasn't ready to be with you. He isn't ready to live for Christ seven days per week. I don't know him and have never seen him, but I feel he's content going to church and coming home. For him it's an act; for you it's a lifestyle. I hear you say y'all have mutual friends and they believed him to be a good man. Don't ever settle for what a person's friends say. He wasn't ready to be with you, and he wasn't going to treat you right.

Unlike his friends and church family, you saw the real him. I heard you say that you blamed yourself and kept wondering what you missed. Can I tell you that God blinded you to who Derek really was and allowed you to marry him? For one thing, God had to allow Derek to marry one of HIS daughters before He corrects him. Number two, you wanted to get married, so God allowed it.

"He also allowed for you to help deliver other women who are going through the same thing. Don't concern yourself with his pastor and first lady not reaching out to you. A lot of churches don't care what their leaders do as long as they are paying tithes. Their leaders can do whatever without any correction. Don't worry; there will be many days he wished he had stayed with you. He may be laughing now, but he will cry later. Be encouraged and do what God told you to do."

Lisa was on the path to forgiving herself. It was as if God were speaking to her at every turn. One night while on Facebook, She saw a post that stated, "What's hardest for a woman isn't losing him. It's forgiving herself for falling in love with his potential, knowing damn well she saw warning signs and his inconsistency." Lisa smiled.

She was sad because Derek was never good to her. He talked about being good, but he didn't execute his goodness. How could she be so stupid to fall in love based off a conversation? He didn't offer anything other than words. That was a sign of desperation. She married someone based off what he said he would do as opposed to his actions. Derek was a talker, not a doer.

The revelation hit, "You don't love yourself." Lisa gasped. "You have low self-esteem. All of these years you have spent alone working on self, praying, fasting, and sowing, the rejected part of Derek appealed to that rejected part of you."

Lisa wasn't yet whole. That was a huge admission. She turned on worship music, got up, walked to the bathroom, and looked in the mirror, "You are fearfully and wonderfully made (Psalm 139:14). You are beautiful inside and out. You are worth love and forgiveness. You are more than enough. You are accepted by the one man, Jesus Christ. You are the apple of your Father's eye. What makes you think that you deserved to be talked down to and belittled? What makes you think that is love? If you loved yourself, you wouldn't have ended up with Derek."

Lisa stopped her confessions long enough to hear, "There is More That I Require of Thee" by Shekinah Glory. All she could do was smile. Lisa admitted, "I hear You, God. What do YOU want me to do?"

"Share your story. It didn't kill you. Share your story with the world."

Lisa said, "Okay, God. I'll grab pencil and paper and begin writing. Thanks for a storyline God. God can turn mess into a message."

To God be the Glory. In the midst of a storm, Lisa saw a rainbow. She had to deal with all of the bystanders who had heard or watched the marriage unfold and knew their curiosity would get the better of them. Lisa asked God for strength as she moved forward because she knew some people would try to keep her attached to Derek. It didn't fail.

The divorce was final and every single person who called inquired to see if Lisa had spoken with Derek. Lisa politely asked her friends to turn the page in that chapter of her life. She asked, "If he wasn't talking to me while we were married, what makes you think he will talk now?" She said, "I told y'all Nabal doesn't believe he has done anything wrong and it's all my fault. Get that boy out of your heads and move forward, because I am."

Most of Lisa's friends respected her wishes. They stopped asking about him, but others would continue to say, "Oh girl, you sound better, because three months ago you were broken." Some of Lisa's friends reminded her of how broken she was on a weekly basis. Believe it or not, Lisa didn't get angry. She was bruised, but not broken.

One of Lisa's closest friends, Tina, from Vicksburg, MS, offered to grab a few of her girls and drive to Arlington, TX, in order to open a can of whoop-ass on Derek. Tina said, "I can get four or five of my girls and we can hop on I-20 West, and it will take us straight to Arlington. We can give him a beatdown and be back home before the night is over."

Lisa laughed and told Tina, "Derek isn't worth it. I feel sorry for him. He's already beaten down but too prideful to see it. He lives in a private hell, but he puts on a good face for the people. He isn't worth the gas or the energy." She thanked Tina for her loyalty. Lisa laughed, because Tina was always willing to whoop someone's assets on behalf of her friends.

Shortly after the divorce, Derek's brother passed away. Family and friends called to see if Lisa would be attending the funeral. Lisa was really shocked. "Are y'all stupid or what?" She and Derek were over. Folks said he needed support. He had family and friends. If Derek talked to Lisa like he had done in the past, there would have been a second funeral. She played the docile wife in order to keep the peace. All bets were off now.

Joyce said, "I'm not suggesting you go to the funeral. I was calling to say, 'Vengeance is mine,' saith the Lord; 'I will repay thee.' He hurt you and now his hurt is coming from another direction."

Lisa said, "I don't know if that's how God operates, but I do appreciate if you don't mention him again. He isn't a factor."

Joyce said, "I bet he's talking about you just like he talked about all of his other women."

Lisa said, "That is fine. He doesn't owe me a thing, but he won't be a part of my daily conversation. I talked about him enough while I was going through it, but that part of my life is over. As a matter of fact, I'm going to take my cousin's advice."

Joyce asked, "What did she say, girl?"

Lisa said, "Sandra told me, 'Don't tell anyone you have been married twice. That fool doesn't count. That was a drive-by marriage and a booty call. No one in your future needs to know about him. The next time you meet a man and he asks how many times you have been married, say once and don't blink. Heck, the only reason I am telling you to acknowledge the first husband is because y'all have children together, but this was a joke, and never mention him again.' "

Joyce and Lisa shared a belly-aching laugh. Joyce agreed, "I guess you're right, but I still don't understand why people can't see he's a big part of the problem."

Lisa didn't respond. That was the last time Joyce talked about Derek. Lisa did think for a fleeting minute to send flowers to the funeral home, but decided that wouldn't be wise.

Chapter Seventeen

Marriage Is a Journey

People will always remind you of where you have been. It was six months after the divorce, but the phone kept ringing with the same inquiries. Lisa eventually had to disconnect from everyone connected to her and Derek. She wrote herself a note and stuck it on the mirror: DON'T DATE ANYONE THAT EVERYONE ELSE KNOWS.

Their little soap opera had ended. Little did anyone know, Lisa never changed her last name. She had the paperwork to do it, but after being informed that Derek wasn't happy, she knew she needed to slow it down. She took two weeks off work in order to do some cleaning and reflecting.

Lisa believed that Derek was punishment for all of her past sins. Derek was the tool God used to teach her a lesson. A lesson unlearned is a lesson returned. She didn't ever want to go through what she went through with Derek ever again. She was in tune with God before Derek. Derek's controlling behavior and self-centeredness caused her to be consumed with what he wanted.

Derek believed he made the decision to move, but God moved him, because he was dangerous to Lisa's growth. Lisa learned that God didn't want anyone or anything to replace HIM, not even a spouse. If she had never told Derek that she didn't trust him, would they still be together? That still, small voice said, "No, Derek never was gone before y'all got started. There was nothing you could have done to save this marriage."

After Lisa heard that voice, there was no more rationalizing what coulda, shoulda, woulda been. The biggest battle Lisa faced was the law of attraction. Since like attracts like, what did that make her? *What character flaws do you have, Lisa? What makes you attract men who don't want to be with you? What area(s) do you need to develop, Lisa?*

Lisa grabbed a tablet and asked a very important question, "How did you marry the same man twenty years apart with different names, but similar personalities?" They were both talkers. They sold themselves very well. They both expressed being a good man. They both took care of the women before her, i.e., paid their bills, car notes, supported their dreams. According to them, the women didn't lack a thing.

Lisa lacked finances with both men, nor were her bills paid. They both blamed their previous girlfriends, fiancées, or wives for the demise of their relationship. Nevertheless, they were both obsessed with their previous relationships. They both lived within five minutes of their exes, whom they loathed. They both hung around women all of the time.

Both men bragged about providing financial support for their mothers (there wasn't any truth to that). Both men lied like rugs. They were ultrasensitive and would lash out. They would do and say things in order to make Lisa feel guilty. The head games were real. The manipulation was real. Lisa cried out to God, "PLEASE reveal and remove anything within me that is attracting these type men, especially the lying part of who I am. Forgive me for every lie I have ever told. Forgive me for being disobedient. Forgive me for every unclean thing that is within me. Forgive me for being incomplete. Forgive me for settling."

Lisa had always made jokes about being the black Elizabeth Taylor. Are both of these failed marriages consequences of those spoken words? She looked up to heaven and said, "Okay, God! I did say I wanted to be the black Elizabeth Taylor, but some things are missing, like the jewelry, money, houses, and cars." Lisa didn't want to get married eight times.

Her marriage takeaways after saying I do twice: domestic abuse and mental illnesses are real. These two components are the reason a lot of marriages end in divorce. There were a lot of people walking around with undiagnosed mental illness. We have to stop justifying by saying, "That's just how I am." Well, you may need a mental health evaluation and possibly medication.

Lisa had been a victim of domestic abuse at the hands of an undiagnosed mentally ill husband. A lot of women are victims of domestic abuse and they suffer in silence, especially if they are married to someone in ministry. Men in ministry use Scripture to keep their spouse in line. "Abuse doesn't have to be physical in order to be destructive. 'The words of his mouth were smoother than butter, but war is in his heart; his words were softer than oil, yet they were drawn swords' (Ps. 55:21). The victim suffers at the hand of the abuser, who professes love but shows hate, who makes inconsistent and contradictory demands from one day to the next. The victim also suffers inconsistent and contradictory advice from fellow Christians." (*Not Under Bondage*, Barbara Roberts, page 16).

Derek professed his love early on but showed hate the duration of the marriage. Don't worry if anyone will believe you. It's your truth and your experience. Victims of domestic abuse often remain silent because the men are typically "good" men in the public eye.

"The perpetrator often presents to the public as a model, mild-mannered citizen—he seems like a good husband. Yet in reality the marriage is characterized by his selfishness, manipulation, and irresponsibility. He lies, minimizes, and twists the truth. If the victim declares the relationship is over, the abuser often wants the relationship to continue and will say so insistently and persistently. He may appear to be deeply sincere and heartbroken. He will often make a show of conversion or recommitment to Christ and/or to counseling when his wife separates. But for all this outward display, he will downplay and minimize his responsibility for the situation and subtly make it look like his wife is at fault" (Barbara Roberts, *Not Under Bondage*, pg. 25).

Remember, Lisa wanted out of the marriage first, but Derek agreed to go to counseling. Derek filed for divorce. Emotional abuse is equally as damaging as physical abuse. The scars from physical abuse can heal. It takes a long time to heal the mind and emotions. Abuse is never okay, not even within the marriage. Lisa had to forgive Derek. Most importantly, Lisa had to forgive herself for allowing Derek to treat her poorly and enabling his demeaning behavior.

LISA'S HELPFUL HINTS

" 'For I hate divorce,' says the Lord, the God of Israel" (Malachi 2:16). God doesn't hate the divorced person(s). God hates the effects of divorce. God created man and the institution of marriage. God doesn't love the institution of marriage more than HE loves the two people within the marriage. I'm not promoting divorce. However, I don't want you feeling condemned to hell because you are divorced. Marriage is beautiful.

Before getting married, it would be wise to learn the purpose of marriage. Marriage has a purpose and it's more than having sex. As a matter of fact, sex is one of the first things to go when the storms come. You have to find common ground outside of the bedroom. How will this marriage survive in the living room or dining room? You and your future spouse will bring your life experiences to the marriage. You and your future spouse will bring your philosophies to the marriage. How will the two operate as one?

Dating is an audition. Reality sets in after the vows. Unrealistic expectations are a big contributing factor to failed marriages. What are your expectations as it relates to being married? What if you are a giver and your future spouse is a taker? Being married to a taker can leave you feeling drained. Do you know your love language?

Do you expect your future spouse to buy you flowers every day? Do you expect to be complimented every day? Do you expect your future spouse to know what you are thinking? Do you expect the two of you will cuddle every night? Do you expect your future spouse to give up all of his/her friends? How well does your future spouse get along with his/her friends? Is he/she a loner or social butterfly? What happens if one of you likes to socialize six days per week but the other one doesn't?

How will you resolve conflict? Will you hold grudges and not talk for days or weeks? Will you text or write notes? Do you expect your future spouse to attend church every time the doors open? Do you expect your future spouse to pray, lead prayer and Bible study at home? Do you expect your spouse to help rear the children, change diapers, etc.?

What about parenting styles? To spank or not to spank? Does your future spouse want children? Will you be a stay-at-home mother? Who will do the household chores? Will it be a joint venture? What if the husband has traditional views, i.e., the wife does everything? What if you are a spender and he's a saver or vice versa? Who will manage the finances? Will you share the same bank accounts?

What are your thoughts about sex? Do you prefer oral sex or vanilla sex? By the way, vanilla sex is missionary only. What happens if you like to travel but your spouse wants to stay home? What happens if you like to go out to dinner but your spouse only likes takeout? What happens if you enjoy going to the movies or dancing, but your spouse's idea of a good time is Netflix and chill seven days per week? Hygiene is important. What if your future spouse has poor hygiene habits? What if he/she has a poor work ethic?

You have to consider generational curses. Family history is important. Family dynamics are huge and can play a role in how well the two of you get along. How important is family to you and your future spouse? How well does your perspective spouse get along with his/her family? What if your spouse's family has a history of mental illness? What about addiction, i.e., pills, alcohol, gambling, sexual addiction, incest, and pornography?

Love is a verb, which means action. Love is the gift that keeps on giving. "Love is patient, love is kind. It doesn't envy, it doesn't boast, it isn't proud. It doesn't dishonor others, it isn't self-seeking, it isn't easily angered, it keeps no record of wrongs. Love doesn't delight in evil but rejoices with the truth. It always protects, always trusts, always hopes, always perseveres" (1 Corinthians 13:4-7).

A lot of people who "love" each other end up getting a divorce. Why? Because we do the opposite of what is written in 1 Corinthians. I love you, but I don't like the way you talk to me. I love you, but I'm not happy with you. I love you, but I'm not in love with you. The feelings of euphoria won't last. They will be fleeting. It's important to establish a friendship. Friendship should be at the core your marriage. If you like your spouse, you can work through the dark days.

Trust, dark days will come. You'll have to find the time to talk about more than your problems. Friends can talk about the weather, current events, sports, religion, fears, and dreams.

This isn't bashing men. However, if more men were taught to be good men first, they would make better husbands. Society and the church teach women to be wives. Most messages and books are geared towards women. Male pastors even target women in their sermons. Men are rarely taught to be husbands.

The message has to be universal. All of us need to understand, marriage is service. Husbands and wives are supposed to serve each other. Too many men have been taught that the wife does all of the serving.

Marriage isn't for the selfish. While you are dating, pay attention to the person who insists on being served. Do they show empathy to others?

Per Pastor Womack, a husband should cherish his wife, regard her highly, be affectionate, engaging, and supportive financially, spiritually, emotionally, and mentally. How many husbands support their wives emotionally? How many husbands are loving? How many husbands understand that God will hold them accountable based on the way they treat their wives? Or do husbands, like everyone else, believe the wives are solely responsible for keeping the marriage together?

Although Kobe Bryant was the "star" of the team, he didn't win those championships alone. The same goes for a marriage. The wife can't do it alone. Marriage is teamwork. Build a strong foundation, and when things get bad, you'll have something to fall back on. Fight for each other, not with each other. Don't forget, marriage needs continual maintenance.

The wedding and honeymoon are an event. Marriage is supposed to be a lifetime commitment. Everyone is worthy of love. Before you say I do, make sure you know what you are getting into. It may be too late after you say I do!

ABOUT THE AUTHOR

Teresa Smith has a passion to help women and to build strong families. She is currently fulfilling this passion as a caseworker for a social services agency and resides in Fort Worth, TX. Teresa earned a master's degree in human services from Liberty University and is also an Army veteran. This is her first book. She hopes to write many more.

Teresa is the loving mother of Demetrius and Malcolm. She is also the loving grandmother of Avery and Jeremiah.

To contact Teresa:

teresasmithbooks@gmail.com
Teresa Smith
PO Box 123812
Fort Worth, TX 76121

www.ingramcontent.com/pod-product-compliance
Lightning Source LLC
LaVergne TN
LVHW021348080426
835508LV00020B/2161